Dearly Departed

A Personal View
of Celebrity Funerals

by

Buddy Galon

authorHOUSE™

1663 LIBERTY DRIVE, SUITE 200
BLOOMINGTON, INDIANA 47403
(800) 839-8640
WWW.AUTHORHOUSE.COM

First published by AuthorHouse 05/26/05

ISBN:1-4208-4194-7 (sc)

Library of Congress Control Number: 2005902478

Printed in the United States of America
Bloomington, Indiana

This book is printed on acid-free paper.

DEDICATION

BEULAH BONDI

"The redoubtable character actress was a wonderful friend and neighbor," says author Buddy Galon. "Of course I attended her memorial service!"

TABLE OF CONTENTS

THE BOOK'S ORIGIN

" 'Allo, Iz theez Boodee Galloon?" asked the woman with a charming accent on the telephone.

"Yes, I am Buddy Galon," I replied.

"Theez iz Lita Baron."

"Yes."

"Lita Baron – you may know me as Mrs. Rory Calhoun."

"Yes, yes, I know who you are."

The lovely Latin actress Lita Baron then proceeded to ask me over the telephone to come to her house the upcoming Friday at eight o'clock in the evening. The occasion was a sit-down black-tie formal dinner. Since I lived on the same street in Beverly Hills, I assured the gracious hostess that I knew where she lived. Who in Hollywood did not know the "Pink Palace" formerly owned by Johnny "Tarzan" Weissmuller and his wife, Mexican actress Lupe Velez?

"Miss Baron," I interrupted her, "Thank you for inviting me; I will be delighted to attend your dinner. However, since you and I don't even know each other, I am curious as to why you are inviting me?"

"Oh!" exclaimed the diminutive movie star. "A mutual psychic acquaintance raved and raved to me about your wonderful funeral stories. Would you please tell some of your funeral stories after the meal at my dinner party?"

Who would have eve guessed that my innocent hobby of attending funerals would lead to being a sought-after guest at movie industry parties. Yes, there I was that Friday evening with screen legend Mae West at one of my elbows and veteran comedian Jimmy Durante at the other. Apparently fascinated by my death tales, they sat in awe, occasionally breaking into laughter, and asking lots of questions.

As we adjourned the dining room, a portly man, then lighting a big cigar, came up to me. Thrusting his book publishing business card into my hand, he simply said, "Kid, you've got a book. Go write it!"

INTRODUCTION

When I was four years old, I watched from a window in my family's home, at a funeral procession to the church next door. My father was the minister so he led the mourners. I found it fascinating! My heartbeat seem to quicken as I witnessed the carrying of the casket by the pallbearers followed by the black-clad family. When the funeral crowd had left, I sneaked over to the empty church. Oh, the fragrance of the flowers, many of which had fallen from the floral arrangements to the floor. Since at that tender age I had no conscious appreciation of aesthetics, what could be causing these special feelings within me?

Have you ever gone to a close relative's funeral? Didn't you experience some unusual feelings? You may say that those feelings only occurred because the dead person was a loved one. However, what about the funerals or memorial services of people that you have never known? I challenge you to deny that the televised funerals of President John F. Kennedy or Princess Diana had absolutely no impact on you.

* * *

When I was only five years old, I would accompany my mother on each Thursday afternoon on her visits to a church member. Mrs. Pruitt always had good cookies and lemonade – I especially liked that about her. However, what was truly wonderful about her was that she lived in a funeral home since her husband was an undertaker. Oh, it was such fun exploring all of those preparation rooms! Where else could a little boy see the draining of blood from a corpse or the inserting of embalming fluid into a dead person?

One day nice Mrs. Pruitt called my mother to ask her to bring me for a special visit that very same day. When we arrived, the mortician's wife led me into the casket display room. Proudly she announced, "Every casket in this room just arrived from the factory this morning. Aren't they lovely?" Mrs. Pruitt gamely lifted me up into the opened caskets so that I could lie down in them. All the while she was blightly praising the various coffins' colors, fabrics, and even the comfort of the mattresses. When I asked, the obliging woman put the lid down as I lay flat in the casket.

Perhaps all of this strikes you as a bit bizarre. However, to a five-year-old lad with no preconceived fear of death, it was just a swell time.

* * *

When I was seven the black preacher in our southern town invited my father, mother and me to a gospel concert at his Afro-American church. It was a life-changing experience. The star attraction of the evening was a magnificent gospel singer named Rosetta Thorpe – a cross between Mahalia Jackson and Ella Fitzgerald. I had never before attended a live musical performance that was so mesmerizing. From that moment on I knew that I wanted music to be a part of my life.

Civil rights advances were unheard of in the South at that time. In a region where separate schools, restaurants, restrooms, and water fountains were firmly entrenched, it must have looked strange to see a small white boy, barefoot in short pants, walking through an all-black neighborhood. To say the least, the sight was uncommon.

Yet that is exactly what happened. When a funeral procession passed the general store where I had just bought a Coca-Cola, I saw the gospel singer Rosetta Thorpe in the car following the hearse. Impulsively I trotted down the dirt road, keeping up with the funeral procession.

At the church I climbed up into the open window, the same place that my father had lifted me up to at that standing-room-only concert of Rosetta Thorpe. The funeral service was of interminable length, but the singing of my new goddess made it all worthwhile.

* * *

By the age of nine I was a seasoned veteran of hearing the hellfire and damnation spewed by funeral preachers and traveling evangelists at church. Perhaps I was too impressionable, but the sermons about burning in hell caused me to have nightmares. Only my tiny black kitten offered me comfort from the fear of eternal flames from the frightening devil. Over and over the church pounded me with the only way to get to Heaven was through public profession of faith and baptism by immersion. Sheer fear made me know that I had to follow the tenets of the church – and soon. Because I loved my tiny black companion so much, I naturally wanted the cuddly kitten to go to Heaven with me. One day after wrapping him completely in an old pillowcase, I immersed Blackie, head and all into a bucket of water. Then for several minutes I mimicked my father's baptismal service ending in "the name of the Father, the Son, and the Holy Ghost." Satisfied that my wonderful pet was now "born again," I lifted him out of the water. He was totally lifeless. How could I have killed the one thing that I loved the most! I cried and cried and cried.

* * *

By my teenage years, I had attended countless funerals – thanks to my father being a minister. Since I had now become an accomplished musician, I was busy playing the piano and the organ with orchestras, for concerts, weddings – and, yes, funerals.

What I liked best about funerals was I got to skip school. You see, I was excused from classes to do the music at morning and afternoon funeral services. Very often I did not know the corpses so before the funerals I would look at them in their caskets and then select my music. For instance, if the deceased was a gruff-looking old man with a handle bar moustache, I might play Wagner marches loudly on the pipe organ. If it were a sweet-looking grandmother type, I might play a syrupy arrangement of "Precious Memories." Oh, and when the corpse was a little baby, I might play lullabies on the piano in high, tinkling notes that multiplied the mourners' tears.

* * *

"Who is it?" demanded the sleepy voice behind the locked door at the Dauphine Street address. It was only a block from noisy Bourbon Street, the heart of New Orleans French Quarter.

"Buddy Galon," was the timid reply.

"Who?" was the impatient response.

"Carmen Carmichael, our boss, sent me here to stay with you while I entertain in his nightclub.

"Carmen sent you! Exclaimed the voice while looking through the peephole. "You don't look like show people; you look like someone on their way to Sunday school. How old are you? Sixteen?

Finally the door opened, and I stood aghast. There in the doorway stood a statuesque platinum blonde stripper named Georgia Lee, wearing gold spike-heeled pumps, a skimpy russet-colored cardigan sweater, and nothing else. The unbuttoned top, barely covering her nipples, contrasted with her being completely naked below the waist. My curious eyes were transfixed on Georgia's southern exposure. After all, I had never seen a woman who shaved down there.

Ignoring the obvious, Georgia stated that it was only seven o'clock in the morning. In fact, she had only stopped stripping on the runway of the Blue Angel three hours ago.

"What time did your plane land, Buddy?" Georgia asked, showing her softer side.

"Two o'clock."

"What have you been doing all that time before you started pounding on my door?"

"Walking in Lafayette Cemetery," I replied.

* * *

If you were observing closely in New Orleans, you might have seen a curly blonde head bobbing up and down among the dark hair of the African-Americans. Yes, it was me who slowly and mournfully sang "Precious Lord, Take My Hand" as the crowd accompanied the coffin to the graveyard. Later I could be seen joining the returning funeral cortege as it snaked its way up Bourbon Street to the very wide Canal Street. I loved the singing and dancing that signaled the end of mourning with the jazz musicians blasting out "When The Saints Go Marching' In."

* * *

Ever since I was a small boy, I suffered from that unique malady called Hollywooditis. Yes, from an early age I knew that someday I was destined to go to Hollywood, California. Well, here I am! I was not certain that I wanted to be in motion pictures or television for a career, but I knew that I was greatly attracted to the entertainment industry.

"Marilyn Monroe, 1926-1962" was the inscription on the bronze plaque of the pink marble crypt illuminated by the headlights of my automobile. I had just driven three thousand miles from Florida to California. After arriving from my long journey, I cruised down famed Hollywood Boulevard that night. Then I drove over to Westwood in search of my new home, the U.C.L.A. branch of the Young Men's Christian Association. How strange it was that on my first night I made a wrong turn onto Glendon Avenue and accidentally discovered the final resting place of Marilyn Monroe!

For a moment I was transported back in time and space to 6:04 in the morning of August 3, 1962. The silence of my Alabama bedroom was pierced by bloodcurdling screams, "Marilyn's dead! Marilyn's dead!

I suddenly sat straight up in my bed. My visibly upset mother then apologized, "I am sorry for waking you up so early in the morning, but I just heard the newscast reporting Marilyn Monroe's death. I knew that you'd want to know."

I did not know her; I never met her. However, the news of her death, for some reason, caused me to feel as if I had been kicked in the stomach. Why does the demise or funeral of a favorite movie star like Marilyn Monroe have such a stunning effect upon seemingly ordinary people?

Each year after I arrived in Hollywood, I went to Marilyn's grave on August 3. There were no formal ceremonies, but a handful of die-hard fans appeared there again and again. Our floral offerings with scribbled messages joined the ever-present six red American Beauty roses that were from former husband Joe DiMaggio.

On the tenth anniversary of the glamorous star's death, I headed toward the cemetery with white daisies – Marilyn's favorite flower. I waited and waited that hot day, but none of Marilyn's faithful fans appeared. On the front page of a major Los Angeles newspaper the next day there was a large photograph of my daisies at Marilyn's grave. The large caption read: TRIBUTE TO A FADED GLAMOR QUEEN. The article continued, "Only a small bouquet of wilted daisies marked the tenth anniversary of the death of Hollywood's greatest glamour queen, Marilyn Monroe. Incidentally, the daisies were accompanied by a note saying, 'I will love you forever. Buddy.'"

Less than three years after Marilyn Monroe's funeral at which Joe DiMaggio banned her friends Peter Lawford, Patricia Kennedy Lawford, and Frank Sinatra, I was now moving freely among the Hollywood set. In fact, I was even entering a close relationship with the flamboyant British noblewoman, Lady May Lawford. You see, I went to tea at her house one day and stayed seven years!

Lady Lawford confided in me that her son actor Peter Lawford and United States Attorney General Robert F. Kennedy were at Marilyn Monroe's home secretly the afternoon of the actress' death. The reason for the house call was purportedly for Kennedy to end his affair with the blonde actress. Waiting for JFK's brother, Bobby, was his wife Ethel and his nine children, staying at the Bates ranch near San Francisco.

The know-it-all Lady Lawford told me, "I felt Peter was awfully mean to Marilyn. After all, on the evening that she died, she had made her last telephone call to him…He could have done something to help her."

She continued, "I knew that Marilyn was seeing Jack Kennedy. I also knew that Marilyn was seeing Bobby Kennedy. They often used Pat and Peter's beach house for their dalliances. Those Kennedys may have done well as a family, but they haven't the faintest idea what discretion means."

"Like I have said before," the outspoken aristocrat repeated, "I like Jack Kennedy. However, I find it difficult to place my complete trust in a President of the United States who always has his mind on his cock."

After a death threat from the Kennedy family, the big-mouthed Lady May Lawford was abducted from her home and silenced forever.

But that's another funeral...

ROSE KENNEDY

Who could have imagined that I would be living in the hotel next door to the St. Edward's Catholic Church! The same St. Edward's Catholic Church that on Friday, January 27, 1995, was the site of the Rose Kennedy memorial service. Many people mistakenly think that this church was built with the Kennedy millions, but the religious edifice was actually the gift of gambler Coloned Edward R. Bradley. Most certainly Rose Kennedy's one dollar offerings did not build or sustain this church. However, for seventy-three winters she did attend daily mass at St. Edward's Catholic Church.

As I sat in pew 143, bearing the inscription that the wooden bench was donated by Mr. and Mrs. William Neil, the motley crowd slowly ambled in. The organist played nondescript music in a stop-and-start manner. In other words, every time that he reached the end of a song, he quit, leaving an awkward silence for about two or three minutes while he changed his music selection. Is this professional?

Sitting directly in front of me at Rose Kennedy's memorial service was a cherub-faced young woman, tented in what appeared to be a well-worn Banana Republic safari outfit. She turned around to me and stared, asking, "Are you somebody?" She then pointed her camera at me. I simply chose to ignore her.

It is reported that the actual funeral for Rose Kennedy had taken place three days earlier at St. Steven Catholic Church in Boston. Forty-three great-grand children, twenty-eight grandchildren, and four surviving children drove in a seventy-mile funeral procession from Hyannisport to the church. As the soaring strains of "Ave Maria" ended, the sole remaining son, Senator Teddy Kennedy, honored his mother with a humorous yet serious eulogy.

Back at the Palm Beach memorial service, hundreds of people who came to pay respects were treated to a rather impersonal occasion. Even the eight-page memorial programs only mentioned the deceased's name once. Of the large crowd present, they would be hard pressed to tell whether the service honored Agnes Schwartz or the matriarch of America's most prominent political dynasty.

Like the rest of the Kennedy family, Rose has been written about ad nauseum – from the birth of Rose Elizabeth Fitzgerald July 22, 1890, on the kitchen table in Boston to her death January 22, 1995, in Hyannisport in her 104th year.

Did you remember that Rose had been named the "National Mother of the Year"? which was a joke since motherhood was really not Mrs. Kennedy's cup of tea. She left the everyday rearing of Joe, Jr., JFK, Rosemary, "Kick," Eunice, Pat, Robert, Jean, and Teddy to an army of governesses, nurses, housekeepers, and cooks.

Upon the demise of her wealthy husband's two-year affair with Hollywood glamour queen Gloria Swanson, Rose grew not only remote but also totally absent. Leaving her young children behind, she traveled abroad seventeen times in six years. When asked about her absences, she said that she needed some new clothes.

Perhaps the award Rose cherished most was to be included on the "Best-Dressed Women in the World" list. Still, she seemed pleasantly pleased upon being recognized as the 'Political Mother of the Year" for having three sons who served as United States senators.

Rose Kennedy was a loner. However, she did have one friend with whom she was rather close. Mary Duncan Sanford, a former actress who married a carpet heir, allowed Rose to swim nude in her swimming pool on a regular basis. This arrangement had to end because Mrs. Sanford's pool was in her living room – over and over her luncheon guests would walk in on a very old and very naked Rose.

The grand dame of the most famous and powerful American political dynasty has not been known to comment on the discovery in the West Palm Beach library. In the downstairs genealogical section there is a large book titled The Blauvert Family Genealogy. In it, socialite Durie Malcolm's 1947 marriage to Congressman John F. Kennedy is listed. Could John F. Kennedy, the first Catholic president, have had a wife before Jacqueline Bouvier?

The Pope bestowed on Rose the title of Papal Countess as the matriarch of the leading Catholic family of America. Could the devoutly religious Rose have been oblivious to her family's raging alcoholism, dangerous drug use, and rampant adultery? It was right there under her roof for decades. Perhaps she turned her head like she did to her husband's blatant infidelities. After all, by keeping quiet, she retained the money and the prestige.

Anyone who knows Rose Kennedy well is aware that she had a passion for eating over-ripe bananas. One morning back in 1984 the already-elderly Rose was waiting to go into daily mass in St. Edward's Catholic Church. Sitting in her old black Cadillac with her chauffeur Dennis in the parking lot, Mrs. Kennedy suddenly had a craving for a dark-skinned banana. Off she tottered on uncomfortable heels to Green's Pharmacy next door. When the headstrong and willful dowager was informed that there were no over-ripe bananas available, she started walking back to her car. Just then she made a sharp left turn, taking her to a large garbage bin. Bending over the bin while standing on her tiptoes, the ageing woman held up a bunch of rotten bananas. Removing one from the bunch, Rose Kennedy – among the wealthiest and most famous women in America – in a designer suit, thousands of dollars in pearls, and large hat returned to her automobile triumphantly carrying a black banana.

The daughter of a congressman, wife of an ambassador, mother of a president and two United States senators, Rose Kennedy is buried in a Holywood Cemetery in Brookline, Massachusetts. She lies next to her philandering husband who died in 1969.

Through three generations of great political triumphs and great personal tragedies, she always reminded us that 'God does not send us a cross any heavier than we can bear."

BARRY GRUNOW

Teacher Barry Grunow fell to the floor mortally wounded.

Student Nathaniel Brazill stood holding the gun.

The students were stunned, screaming, and running for cover.

About 3:25 on Friday afternoon, May 30, 2000 – the last period of the last day of school – a popular English teacher was gunned down in full view of his class. At Lake Worth Middle School, only a few blocks from where I reside, a former honor student, using a stolen pistol, shot the teacher in the face.

Barry Grunow was a thirty-five-year-old Caucasian school teacher who was well-liked by students, parents, and faculty. Devoted to his wife and two children, Grunow loved teaching and playing basketball.

Nathaniel Brazill was a thirteen-year-old seventh grader who was known as both polite and truthful. Brazill, an Afro-American, was a regular churchgoer with his mother, Mrs. Polly Powell. In fact, the Brazill family spokesman was Rev. Thomas Masters, the rabid civil rights activist.

Never have I had to stand in line for a long time to get into a funeral. Not even for a movie star funeral at the famous but tiny Kirk of the Heather chapel at Forest Lawn. Scores of us waited in the heat and humidity for the doors of Good Shepherd Methodist Church to open for the 11:00 a.m. memorial service.

This was no ordinary funeral for Lake Worth, Florida, a small town just across the bridge from affluent Palm Beach. Hundreds of mourners were adolescents – many attending a death service for the first time.

Instead of wearing black, the young people were a mass of blue jeans, micro-mini skirts, tattoos, piercings, blue and neon-colored hair. However, although the murder occurred four days before, the students' faces were

4

still etched with horror and grief. Throughout the sanctuary were group of students huddled together sharing their tears.

When Barry Grunow was a child, he would collect bugs from the neighbors' yards and keep them in a jar. Not wanting to steal the bugs, Barry left pennies in their place. These were the words of Kurt Grunow at the memorial service of his brother. Oldest brother Steve Grunow recalled how a young Barry picked his dog Wilma from the pound "because she was the ugliest dog there and if he didn't take her, nobody else would."

The Reverend Bill Corristan stood behind a bank of flowers, a huge picture of Grunow and collages of family snapshots. Three busloads of Lake Worth Middle School teachers sat there united in their last farewell to their fellow teacher. During more than one hour, the service dragged on dominated by the monotonous recordings of Jethro Tull, the deceased's favorite singer. The traditional hymn Amazing Grace ended the funeral service.

The celebration of the life of the students' "hero" and "everybody's favorite teacher" was attended by at least 1650 students, faculty, family and townspeople. It is interesting to note that Afro-Americans made up about half of the number of mourners.

The shot that was fired set into motion immediate action. A "Stop the Violence Rally" and a march against weapons were held at Bryant Park within hours after the shooting. Hundreds attended. While youths were still placing flowers, cards, and stuffed animals on the school fence, the Palm Beach School Board sent thirty-five grief therapists to counsel students and school personnel. Churches, both white and black, held special prayer services. One thousand persons attended the candlelight vigil at John Prince Park.

However, the shocked small community was not prepared to deal with the outside world, especially the media hordes. Time, CNN, People magazine, The New York Times, and even a Japanese news organization arrived immediately. ABC network's Good Morning, America and CBS network's The Early Morning Show were not far behind NBC's Today Show with their live telecasts from Lake Worth. Before the media spectacle faded, 136 news organizations focused the unblinking eye at extensive national media attention upon the small town of Lake Worth.

Meanwhile, the local Center for Family Services offered free therapy to teachers and their families suffering from this tragedy. Lake Worth Middle School announced a gun-safety seminar for the public. A free trigger lock was to be given as a gift to all who attend. Later slain teacher Barry Grunow's widow filed suit against the distributor of the cheap handgun used to kill her husband on the last day of school.

Pam Grunow was quiet and unexpressive in the same loose-fitting pale blue print dress that she wore to each of the public events connected to her husband's death. A memorial fund was set up at a local bank to assist Pam and her small children. A college trust fund was begun to assure higher education for the little boy and girl. In an emotional decision the Palm Beach County School Board gave Grunow's widow her dead husband's salary and benefits for seventeen years. Meanwhile, the slain English teacher's pals paid tribute to him with a basketball tournament raising thousands of dollars for a Grunow college scholarship. School children at his school established the new gymnasium in his name. Both Lake Worth Middle School and Florida Atlantic University now boasted of a Barry Grunow Butterfly garden.

It was all a bittersweet memory. Just a single shot from a student's gun on May 26, 2000, catapulted Barry Grunow into a national symbol of escalating school violence; a tragic tale of a good husband, a good father, and a good teacher lost.

On May 16, 2001 Barry Grunow's seemingly unremorseful student, now 14, was found guilty of second-degree murder. Twenty-two years to life in prison is killer Nathaniel Brazill's possible penalty.

MARSHA MAY

After I signed my name in the family registry at the ultra-modern Gutterman-Warheit Memorial chapel, I followed Marsha May's husband, stepchildren, her mother, and her brother into the sanctuary for the 10:30 morning service. From the mortuary located on the Boca Raton, Florida, city limits the funeral caravan snaked its way to the Boca Raton Mausoleum for entombment. The door on the life of Marsha May appeared to close on August 27, 2001.

I first met pretty Marsha May at the office of The Palm Beach Post. She had begun her journalism career at that newspaper as a lowly reporter in 1970. Now more than ten years later she was playing hostess to me – a winner of the newspaper sponsored writing competition.

We all appreciated Marsha's unique writing style. In fact, that style caught the eye of pretty blond former actress Lois Pope who, in turn, brought Marsha to the attention of her husband. He was not just any old husband – he was the rich and powerful Generoso Pope, Jr., publisher of the top tabloid The National Enquirer.

Lovely Lois Pope gently begged her husband to give Marsha a chance. When he gave the young writer a tryout column in his current publication, she and her column were an instant hit. One week later Marsha May was hired by The National Enquirer as their first female writer.

"Tales of True Courage," a weekly column profiling people in crisis, was Marsha's popular tabloid feature. She was enjoying high-paying journalism for the first time. Before long she was promoted to associate editor, which catapulted her into bigger money. Finally she worked on the tabloid's front-page stories including the two largest-selling issues in tabloid history: the death of Elvis Presley and the fatal accident of Princess Grace.

Marsha May was now reputed to be the highest-paid female journalist in America. Yet in 1989 she found love, and kissed her writing career good-bye. She was rich and a Life Master in bridge, and he was rich and a Life Master in bridge. It appeared to be a marriage made in heaven. Together Dr. and Mrs. James Sternberg became newlyweds who traveled the entire world both playing and winning bridge tournaments.

Of all the countries they visited, the couple chose Italy as their favorite. There Marsha could indulge her passion for sailing, play spirited games of tennis, and polish off 18 holes of golf. Still, tournament bridge was the major attraction for both of them. Eventually Dr. Sternberg arranged his schedule so that he and his wife could live in Italy every spring and every summer.

Marsha and James Sternberg did more than just reside in Italy. They took their combined riches and made a significant difference in the lives of the Italian people. In recognition of their philanthropic efforts in their country, the Sternbergs received the titles of the Count and Countess of Abruzzi. They became known as Contesssa Marcella Berghini and Conte Giacamo Berghini to nobility, the social set, and the Italians.

Cancer claimed Marsha May Sternberg at the age of fifty-three. Although her widower, Dr. Sternberg, remained a professor of radiology at the University of Minnesota, he has annually organized fund-raising tournaments in her memory.

LOIS DAY MEACHAM

Have you made that important visit to your funeral home or cemetery yet? Death is inevitable so perhaps you need to consider pre-need arrangements. What about the selection of a casket or an urn? Funeral services? Memorial services? Flowers? Special music? Do you honestly wish to burden relatives with all of these arrangements? And, perish the thought, what if those close relatives are totally lacking in responsibility or are harboring some past grudge?

All of these questions lead up to the situation of my neighbor and dear friend Lois Meacham. Our residences were back-to-back one block from the beach in downtown Palm Beach. When I first met her in the early 1980s, we were both strolling along the beach in the late afternoon. Although her face remained pretty and unlined, Mrs. Meacham was quick to remind me that the infirmities of age and disease were fast ravaging her body.

Over tea or while devouring her favorite Belgian waffles or just sitting on a bench facing the Atlantic Ocean, we shared many conversations concerning her limited future. A believer in pre-need arrangements, Mrs. Meacham was still no foolish consumer. She felt that the funeral seller is preoccupied with price and profit made from impulse buyers or guilty, remorseful, grieving family members. The lovely lady laughed at the attempts of undertakers to sell her dainty footwear for after-death and a super-soft mattress for her casket. She challenged Service Corporation International (SCI), the giant octopus controlling the prices of the funeral industry, by demanding an itemized list of her pre-need funeral costs. They refused.

The end of Lois Meacham's life was gradually approaching as the years went by. She only got out of bed once a day – to hobble on her cane over to Merrill Lynch to check on her stock portfolio.

"Do you know what my favorite part of the newspaper is?" Mrs. Meacham asked me one day. "The obituaries. I especially like the interesting manner in which the Palm Beach newspaper presents the summation of the lives of the newly deceased," the attractive lady answered her own question.

Continuing her train of thought, Lois Meacham requested that I write her obituary for the Palm Beach newspaper upon her death. At first I hesitated, but I finally agreed after I could see how much it meant to her. Then she went over all the material that she wished to be written about her at the time of her demise.

A brief telephone call came from Mrs. Meacham just before she died. I assured her that I would write her obituary as I had promised. Whereupon the proud woman once again went over the information to be included. At the end of the conversation she thanked me for giving her peace of mind; she told me that she loved me, and said, "Good-bye." Her death was immediate.

Here is the obituary that Mrs. Meacham wanted printed in the Palm Beach newspaper:

LOIS DAY MEACHAM

Distantly related to the Rockefellers, the Astors, and the Phipps families, Lois Day Meacham departed this earth late yesterday at her Palm Beach residence.

The daughter of Ernestine and Julian Day, Miss Day was born in Winchester, Massachusetts and educated at Erasmus Hall. After her marriage to George Meacham of Sewickly, Pennsylvania, the young couple went to live at Beekman Place in New York City.

While singing and acting in Vincent Youman's Productions on Broadway, Lois Day Meacham enjoyed a circle of friends that included Admiral Byrd, General Jimmy Doolittle, Admiral Rickenbacker and Charles Lindbergh. At one point in her life she was closest companion to horseman Alfred Gwynne Vanderbilt, attending all of the Saratoga races with him.

Among her clubs and affiliations were the St. Mary's Guild at Bethesda-by-the-Sea Episcopal Church, the Bath and Tennis Club, and the American Yacht Club of Marblehead, Massachusetts.

Surviving Lois Day Meacham are two daughters: Baroness Jacque de Rothchild of Rochemont, Switzerland, and Mrs. Andrew Carnegie III of Palm Beach. Also three grandchildren.

Mrs. Meacham's well-planned obituary was removed from the Palm Beach newspaper office on the angry demand of an inebriated member of her family. In its place was a terse death notice of very few words printed at the bottom of the newspaper's page. Will a spiteful relation keep you from having a decent obituary?

When I went to visit Lois Day Meacham's grave, a place that she had selected years before, she was not buried there.

Will a hateful relative rob you of your final resting place?

PRINCESS NINA MDIVANI

Once upon a time in the faraway province of Georgia in Russia, General Zachary Mdivani, former aide-de-camp to Czar Nicholas II and Elizabeth Sobolevska, a Polish fortuneteller, met and married. Five children resulted from this union – Nina, Serge, David, Roussadana, and Alexis. In time, all of the five children must have kissed the fabled frog because they each turned into princes and princesses. Yet the Mdivanis were not landowners so they were not qualified in Georgia to be titled.

The oldest sister Princess Nina Mdivani helped her family's cause by marrying Charles Henry Huberick, an international lawyer whose entire practice would eventually handle the family's many legal matters – especially divorce and estate settlements.

The other sister was the amoral Princess Roussadana, who lived in a ménage a trios arrangement with artists Misia and Jose Maria Sert. She was the schemer who hatched the plot that led her three brothers down the path of lucrative matrimony. It was her idea to offer the common oil rig workers as titled, handsome, athletic, great lovers to the wealthy woman. These beefy grooms for hire soon became known as "the marrying Mdivanis."

Prince David Mdivani was the first brother to stalk debutantes, heiresses, rich divorcees, wealthy widows, and movie stars. After dumping famous movie star Pola Negri for Mae Murray, the big star of "The Merry Widow." David quickly stripped Miss Murray of three million dollars of savings. She wound up homeless living on a bench in Central Park. Later, David fleeced oil heiress Virginia Sinclair for more than a million dollars.

Prince Serge Mdivani, seemingly jealous of his brother David's newly-acquired life of luxury, married his brother's former fiancée, actress

Pola Negri. Three million dollars of her money had disappeared during their brief marriage. The pompous Serge then wed opera singer Mary McCormick and went through her two-million-dollar nest egg within three months.

Along came the third arrogant and non-feeling Mdivani – Prince Alexis Mdivani. His first marriage was to Standard Oil heiress Louise Van Alen. Before the honeymoon had ended, the snobbish phony prince purchased himself a custom-made Rolls Royce and an expensive string of polo ponies from her checking account. Less than eighteen months later Alexis married Woolworth heiress Barbara Hutton who had recently inherited $42,077,327.53.

I first met Princess Nina, the most senior of the Mdivani siblings, in the mid-1960s. Somehow I found myself in the middle of a love-hate relationship between the volatile princess and an equally volatile Lady May Lawford. Despite their differences, they always maintained a loyal friendship.

Nearly ten years later I reported to a Palm Springs location where a live NBC radio show was to be broadcasted. My contract was as music director for the show "The Cocktail Party" starring Arthur Lake and his wife Patty. Was Lady Lawford gossiping when she told me that Arthur (Dagwood) Lake's wife Patty was the illegitimate daughter of publisher William Randolph Hearst and his mistress, actress Marion Davies? Anyway, sitting against the wall between model Marilyn Visel and columnist Sally Presley was Princess Nina Mdivani. Age had caught up with her: unkempt gray hair, nearly blind, and a plump, lumpy body that her black dress did not hide.

On Tuesday, March 3, 1987, Princess Nina, the last surviving member of the Georgian clan of Mdivanis, died in London. She was believed to be in her late eighties.

Some three months later I attended her memorial services in Edinburgh, Scotland. The formal morning services featured excellent pipe organ music along with bagpipes. However, the heavy Scottish brogue prevented me from understanding the eulogist well.

Princess Nina Mdivani's last husband, Dennis Conan Doyle, predeceased her. Taking a page from the lives of her brothers who married into fame and fortune, the dead woman lived handsomely from the estate of her father-in-law Sir Arthur Conan Doyle, the creator of Sherlock Holmes. By the way, the memorial services took place at St. Giles Cathedral – across from Arthur Conan Doyle's birthplace.

JOSEPHINE DILLON

Socialite-writer-actress Lady May Lawford was missing from her Beverly Hills residence. Foul play was suspected in the mysterious disappearance of the aristocratic widow of war hero Sir Sydney Lawford and mother of actor Peter Lawford. When I joined the search for Lady Lawford, I went from nursing home to nursing home. As I was walking into a Glendale sanitarium, the dead body of famed drama coach Josephine Dillon was being carried out.

Back in 1920 Josephine Dillon, already a respected figure in the theatre, was having trouble with the telephone in her Portland, Oregon home. A strapping telephone lineman came to repair her phone.

She later told friends, "He had terribly decayed teeth and such big ears, but we started a conversation. He asked me, 'I wanna try acting, and I just wondered if you would help me?'"

"He was such a grateful pupil. I had to start at the very beginning with him, get his teeth pulled and have false ones put in."

She not only had his teeth pulled, but she also married him that same year – despite the fact that she was sixteen years older. Together as Mr. And Mrs. Clark Gable they headed for Hollywood, California.

In the nation's film capital Josephine continued to teach Clark everything that he came to know about acting. She spent week after week, month after month, and year after year training Clark Gable in diction, body movement, projection, use of keylight, camera angles, cinematic naturalness, and all the techniques of the craft.

The next ten years were the happiest of Josephine's life. She was pleased to use her considerable influence with movie studios to get film roles for Clark. When his motion picture stardom was assured, Clark Gable walked out on his marrige without explanation. His next wife was Rita Langham, another older woman who offered him money and social prestige. This appeared to establish a pattern – marrying wealthy socialites – most of Clark's life.

After their 1930 divorce, Clark Gable did not ever speak to or see his first wife – although she had more to do with making him one of the biggest stars in Hollywood than any other person. In 1957, three years before his death of a heart attack, Gable sent a lawyer to offer Miss Dillon $6,000 for her $100,000 Hollywood house. Alone, ill, in debt, and desperately in need of money, Josephine signed the house over to Clark. It was not much later that a confused Miss Dillon was committed to the Glendale sanitarium where she remained until her death.

How soon they forget. There were only eighteen people who attended the rather generic funeral service at the small chapel on Raymond Avenue in Pasadena.

A famous drama coach and a forgotten relic of the great star Clark Gable's past, Josephine Dillon apparently outlived her fame. In fact, it looked as if the eighty-seven year old former acting teacher had even outlived many of her pupils who included Colleen Moore, Mary Astor, Lupe Velez, Rochelle Hudson, Leslie Howard, Johnny Weissmuller, Bruce Cabot, Cary Grant, and John Wayne. Many of them owed their movie careers to her.

As her life was ebbing to an end, Miss Josephine Dillon told friends that "Clark Gable was my first and only husband, and when we meet in heaven, we'll be together again, as Mr. And Mrs. Clark Gable."

P.S. After leaving the funeral, I found a kidnapped Lady May Lawford hidden away in a Raymond Avenue convalescent hospital, only two blocks away.

DARRYL ZANUCK

"You are absolutely wrong," said the person sitting next to me as we were driving on Wilshire Boulevard in Los Angeles to Darryl Zanuck's funeral. "The service obviously is going to be at the temple up ahead on the left." I refused to admit that I was wrong: "You mistakenly think that Zanuck was Jewish like all the other Hollywood movie moguls. He was Swiss Protestant." After we stopped at the deserted temple, I smugly steered the car further down the hill a few hundred yards on the right. There was an impressive number of mourners gathering outside of the United Methodist Church.

Darryl Francis Zanuck was born on September 5, 1902, in Wahoo, Nebraska, the son of Swiss parents. When a health condition developed, eight-year-old Darryl moved to Los Angeles where he skipped school to break into the movies. The boy, dressed in the costume of an Indian maiden, earned one dollar a day at a local studio.

Quitting school in the eighth grade, Darryl joined the army when he was only fourteen years old. He was primarily a messenger because of his 5'6" height and 142 pounds weight. His small size next led him into a bantamweight-boxing career.

A letter that Zanuck wrote to <u>Stars and Stripes</u>, the armed forces newspaper, determined Zanuck's permanent career. The prose of his writing made him head for Hollywood. There his job of selling hair tonic catapulted him into writing for the movies. The young writer was hired to write films for the dog star Rin Tin Tin, but soon he claimed himself being responsible for the first talking picture in 1928, <u>The Jazz Singer</u> with Al Jolson.

For the next fifty years Darryl Zanuck managed to survive the precarious motion picture industry as a highly-paid executive producer.

Eventually he became the combative president of the Twentieth Century-Fox movie studio. Along the way he claimed responsibility for such successful and well-remembered films as The Grapes of Wrath, Winged Victory, The Razor's Edge, and Gentlemen's Agreement. Even toward the end of his career, he was partly responsible for hits such as Patton, M.A.S.H., Butch Cassidy and the Sundance Kid, and The Sound of Music.

I first saw Darryl Zanuck in the mid-1960s. He was in the process of establishing a polo ground out of what appeared to be a potato patch. It was a curious sight as I watched from the place where I stayed on the main street, South Palm Canyon Drive in Palm Springs, California. An even more curious sight was when Zanuck, parading in full polo regalia that included knee-high riding boots, helmet, and riding crop, came into our neighborhood coffee shop, Lindy Lou's. Despite the movie mogul's peculiar attire, he still couldn't outdo Lindy Lou's most noticeable customer: old-time glamour queen Norma Shearer heavily made-up and draped in pastel clothes apparently designed by her late husband Arrouge.

Who would have thought that by the late 1960s I would be under protégé contract at 20th Century-Fox studio where Darryl Zanuck was boss. Legendary producer Adolph Zukor, nearly 100 years old, took me under his wing planning to mold me into another Cary Grant. Not a chance! My respect for Darryl Zanuck hit rock bottom when I learned that his fabled "casting couch" was a reality. I knew several actresses who were pressured by Zanuck to be his "sex slave" if they wanted to continue working at the studio.

However, it is with son Richard Zanuck, the studio veep, that I have a bone to pick. Years ago I was musical director of a national beauty pageant held in a southern state. Young Dicky Zanuck, representing his daddy's studio, flew in from Hollywood to judge the pageant. He promptly picked an underage beauty to be in his own personal contest in his own bed. Why does this concern me? Because I had a major crush on the newly deflowered young miss since we first appeared together at age six in a talent contest. Apparent studio and parental pressures soon forced the junior movie executive to rush back, collect the girl, put her in a movie, introduce her as actress Lili Gentle, marry her in a big wedding – all before their baby arrived!

My last brush with this powerful family was Mrs. Darryl Zanuck, surely the most gracious member of the movie dynasty. As luck would have it, the Zanuck mansion in Palm Springs was across the street from the building where I spent considerable time working on a book about the area's educational history. First known as actress Virginia Fox and as

Buster Keaton's favorite leading lady, Mrs. Zanuck now simply enjoyed caring for her three grown children and puttering in her garden. She has always held her head high despite her embarrassment concerning her husband's multitudinous flings and longtime public affairs with Juliette Greco and Bella Darvi.

The high point at Darryl Zanuck's funeral should have been the beautiful and eloquent eulogy delivered by Hollywood's resident movie genius, Orson Welles. However, the excellent oratory was overshadowed by his attempt to enter the pulpit of the church. The grossly obese Welles, like a great beached whale, became stuck in the swinging wooden doors for a few moments in front of the many amused mourners.

Two actors were standing on the church steps following Zanuck's funeral. One said to the other: "I never expected to see you here honoring Zanuck after he sabotaged your career a few years back." The other responded, "Oh, I still hate the son of a bitch. By the way, I didn't attend his funeral to honor him – I only came to make certain he was really dead!"

DOLLY SINATRA

Graduation Day at Pepperdine University had been especially beautiful. The outdoor commencement with its awarding of college degrees was almost overshadowed by the roaring blue ocean waves of Malibu. The very next morning, armed with my new Master's Degree diploma, I drove out to Palm Springs to land a position in the field of education. At my job interview with the school official that day I accepted low-paying entry-level employment knowing that this job was merely an immediate steppingstone to a higher position. As I drove away from the interview in my automobile, the school official shouted after me, "If that's your Rolls Royce, do you really want this job?"

Looking down at my watch, I realized that I had exactly twenty minutes. Yes, exactly twenty minutes to get to the funeral of Dolly Sinatra, singer Frank Sinatra's mother. I drove up to the rather ugly church in the rather ugly neighborhood as the ushers were locking the front doors.

I ran toward the locking church doors. "Wait a minute!" I shouted at the ushers. Once at the entrance, I was asked whose party I was a member of. I hesitated a moment – then remembering that I had a seven-year relationship with Lady May Lawford, Peter's mother – I quickly said, "The Peter Lawford party." I was whisked to The Family section. My row-end seat was beside Sammy Davis Jr. If I had stretched out my right arm, I would have touched Frank Sinatra.

Dolly Sinatra was solemnized and memorialized with a requiem mass at St. Louis Roman Catholic Church in Cathedral City, a suburb of Palm Springs. This is the church that Dolly attended in her later years. Frank Sinatra spent thousands and thousands of his money on his mother's funeral. Who would have believed that the funeral music could be so mediocre when her son Frank was an international power in the music industry! Graveside services were held for Dolly at Desert Memorial Park with composer Jimmy Van Heusen, actor-singer Dean Martin, baseball great Leo Durocher, comic Pat Henry, and restaurateur Jilly Rizzo carrying the expensive bronze casket.

The conditions that accompanied Dolly Sinatra's death colored her funeral. On January 6, 1977, Dolly was flying to Las Vegas to gamble and to attend her son's nightclub opening. The private Lear jet taking Mrs. Sinatra from Palm Springs to Las Vegas crashed into a snow-covered mountain. Within hours son Frank was searching for his mother when a search pilot saw her body pieces and Dolly's large flowery muu muu attached to the limb of a mountain tree. The flying of Mrs. Sinatra in the airplane seemed to touch off illusions of soaring angels at the funeral service. Mother Sinatra, in the requiem mass, received the laudatory remarks usually reserved for Mother Theresa.

Born Natalie Garavante, a Hoboken, New Jersey girl of Italian descent, "Dolly" was a plump blue-eyed blond elementary school dropout. As a tough, ambitious teenager, she married a Sicilian boxer named Marty Sinatra who later became a fireman. On December 12, 1915, the Sinatras became the parents of their only child, a son named Francis Albert Sinatra. This began the lifelong love-hate relationship between Frank and the mother who violently opposed her son being a singer.

Dolly Sinatra, both loudmouthed and foulmouthed, achieved quite a reputation early in her life. Her notoriety first came from her part in an ongoing political vote corruption machine; later she was involved in crooked court practices. These frauds were overshadowed by her actions that led her to be called "The butcher of Hoboken." An abortionist, she killed babies for $25.00 each on a table in her basement. When confronted, the woman explained, "But I did not use a clothes hanger, I used a long wire."

As I sat observing Frank Sinatra's mother's funeral, I wondered what church provides a requiem mass for a convicted baby killer. Doesn't that church prohibit abortion? Or does money alter certain decisions by the church?

Frank Sinatra was profoundly affected by Dolly's death. She was the most important person in his life, and he especially wanted to please her. When Frank thought that he had finally bought his way into the Knights of Malta, supposedly the oldest and most exclusive social order of chivalry in the world, the doting son knew this great honor would please his mama.

When his friend, convicted Mafia murderer Jimmy "The Weasel" Fratianno offered to get Frank into the Red Knights, a division of the Catholic organization that did not require Vatican approval for induction, the singer was thrilled to write a ten thousand dollar check for his membership.

The entire Red Knights was a fraudulent scheme. Frank excitedly accepted fake scrolls and medals from the fictitious organization. He even proudly flew his pseudo Knights of Malta flag over his Palm Springs home and gave his wife Barbara a Maltese cross to show off when in public. A phony induction to Knighthood, possibly featuring Prince Petrucci of Italy and Prince Bernhard of Holland, had Frank puffed up about his imagined exalted station in life. Dolly's airplane crashed before the sham investiture took place so she never knew of his pseudo knighthood or how the Mafia had made a fool of him.

After Dolly's death, Frank began attending mass – something that he had not done for six decades. He even hired an in-house Catholic priest to offer him twenty-four hour attention. The aging Chairman of the Board and former leader of the irreverent Rat Pack now decided that he wanted to return to the sacraments so he devised a plan.

The plan that he devised would honor his mother's memory and also get her forgiveness for his marrying Barbara Marx, a Protestant, six months before the plane crash in a non-Catholic ceremony. Simply, the plan itself was his intention to remarry Barbara in front of a Catholic priest. Then he could take Holy Communion and the state of his soul would be heaven bound, or so he thought

Barbara Marx Sinatra, the former Las Vegas showgirl, was the easiest part of The Plan. She willingly agreed to take the necessary instructions for a Catholic marriage ceremony. However, the annulment of his 1939 marriage to Nancy Barbato in Our Lady of Sorrows Catholic Church was more troublesome since it was seen as valid in the eyes of the church. There was also a little matter that this marriage produced three children.

Princess Lee Radziwill, sister of Jacqueline Kennedy Onassis, and the ruling Grimaldi family had persuaded the Vatican to grant their various annulments. This gave Frank hope that a wafer and a sip from the communion cup would soon be his. How convenient that there was no need to annul his second marriage to actress Ava Gardner and his third marriage to actress Mia Farrow because those had not been performed in the Catholic church and therefore were not recognized as valid.

Along came the revised Code of Canon Law which allowed him easily to dissolve his first marriage and re-wed Barbara by a Catholic priest. Now Frank Sinatra could honor his mother's memory, and his apparition of his death, and save himself from eternal damnation.

Frank's annulment was not without question. Joseph M. Kelly wrote, "The fact that Sinatra obtained this annulment three marriages after a valid marriage many years ago in the church to a Catholic lady who bore him three children raises many questions in the eyes of Catholics and non-Catholics alike. Did his power and influence play a role in this annulment?"

Alas, what about the children – Nancy, Jr., Frank, Jr., and Tina? The grown-up two daughters and one son were understandably horrified at their father's secret plan. Just in time, a 1977 revised church canon stated that an annulment no longer does anything to affect legitimacy or the laws of inheritance. The three children were saved from being called bastards. Whew!

HARRY RICHMAN

Cincinnati, Ohio was the birthplace in 1895 of this future musical star. By age twelve he was performing in vaudeville in blackface. World War I interrupted his budding career while he served in the United States Navy.

Reviving his musical career in his early twenties, Harry Richman was the accompanist for Mae West and the Dolly sisters in their New York productions.

"Club Richman," on ritzy Park Avenue, was his very own pre-Prohibition speakeasy that gave the performer even more fame. In the meantime, he was appearing in *Varieties of 1922, Queen of Hearts*, and the *George White Scandals of 1926*.

During the 1930s Harry Richman literally moved his address to Broadway appearing in show after show, from *Sons O'Guns* with Lili Damita to the *Ziegfield Follies* to *Say When* with Bob Hope.

Richman then appeared in several Hollywood movies, but he could never top one of his earliest and one of his most successful film musicals: *Putting on the Ritz*.

While he was having a well-publicized on-again-off-again affair with the "It girl" Clara Bow, he was cementing his fame with a nightly national radio broadcast originating from his New York nightclub.

For two decades Harry Richman packed the palladium in London, the Café de Paris in Monte Carlo as well as the Palace, Roxy, Capitol, and the Paramount theatre in New York City. Don't forget the Desert Inn in Las Vegas.

Yvonne must be his favorite female name – he married model Y vonne Epstein and dancer Yvonne Day. In between he also wed Ziegfeld Follies beauty Hazel Froidebaux. After three tempestuous and expensive marriages the entertainer later enjoyed the companionship of his pet squirrel as he lived out a stingy retirement.

When Harry Richman died at seventy-seven years of age in Burbank, California, his star had long since dimmed. Few recalled the song-and-dance man of the crisp tuxedo, the straw boater hat, and his cane.

However, there are some old-timers who remember when Harry was one of the highest-paid performers on Broadway. They haven't forgotten that Harry was a bigtime playboy with lots of beautiful showgirls, a dangerous yen for gambling, and a love of amateur aviation. These elderly fans of Harry were divided when it came to voting on their favorite of Harry's songs: "Puttin' on the Ritz" or "Walking My Baby Back Home."

The day of the Jewish funeral service in Hollywood for Harry Richman, there were no adoring fans. After all, it was 1972 – decades after his glittering stardom. His four remaining closest friends – Eddie Cantor, Ben Bernie, George Jessel, and Ruby Vallee – were there to mourn their dear friend.

After George Jessel, "the eulogist to the stars," delivered a rather dry and a rather lengthy appraisal of the deceased, the dark wooden casket was closed.

His familiar straw hat and his ever-present cane were placed on the casket while in the background was heard the recorded voice of Harry Richman singing his famous hit, "On the Sunny Side of the Street."

I won't lie to you – I left the service with tears in my eyes and a lump in my throat.

"ZANE"

"I have got AIDS!" the male voice sobbed into the telephone mouthpiece. My first inclination was to hang up on the virtual stranger making the most personal confession. But I didn't.

It was the "wrap party" for an independent motion picture made in the early 1980s about a boy named Scooter. The less-than-successful movie was filmed completely in the West Palm Beach, Florida, area. Thus, it didn't require too much imagination for the party celebrating the end of production of this dubious contribution to cinematic art to take place at a West Palm Beach gin mill masquerading as a trendy disco.

Entering the party fashionably late, I somehow felt overdressed in my trademark white suit. My position as president of the Florida Motion Picture and Television Association and my entertainment column in the local movie-TV newspaper made me somewhat of a minor celebrity. People often surrounded me in public. After a few inane conversations and a couple of bites of well-prepared rumaki, I looked around the crowded, noisy room for a place to sit down. That's when curvaceous opera singer Janna Howard and her handsome escort offered me a seat at their postage stamp-sized table.

Several nights later the telephone in my apartment rang. The anxious and excited voice on the other end belonged to the young man who was with diva Janna Howard at the aforementioned party. Our meeting had been so fleeting that I did not even remember his name.

"Hello, Buddy, this is Zane – the guy who escorted Janna Howard to the party the other night. In the few minutes that we talked at the party, you impressed me as a kind, compassionate man. I badly need such a person to talk to tonight," He pleaded.

He then asked to meet him at an out-of-the-way restaurant that hugged the seacoast about halfway between the towns that we each lived in. I struggled to think of a logical excuse to get out of meeting Zane that night. However, my ability to lie was at an all-time low. Yes, I agreed to meet him.

As I grudgingly drove to the small eatery where I was to meet Zane (not his real name), I thought about my brief meeting with him last week. Didn't I think that he was homosexual? Still, I hate myself for jumping to snap decisions about other people's sexuality. I didn't like it when people made such instant judgments about me. Oh well, I had been a part of the Hollywood film industry for nearly a quarter of a century so I certainly knew how to handle any situation dealing with homosexuality.

"I have got AIDS! Zane repeated his exact pronouncement from his earlier telephone call. My fork dropped into my salad – not to be lifted again. Zane continued, "I thought that I might have hypoglycemia, a blood sugar disorder, but my doctor told me today that I am diagnosed as having acquired immune deficiency syndrome. Not only that, the doctor says that I am in the early stages of pneumocystic carinii, a type of pneumonia that will cause my death within a few months." Listening to Zane, I was both numb and speechless. Perhaps that was best; the young man was able to talk out his dilemma without interruption.

He does not look like a man who will die of AIDS. The healthy tan, the muscular physique underneath the tailored sport clothes, and the ready smile belie what is happening inside his body.

Zane bravely went about telling his family immediately. First he notified them of his impending death of AIDS, and at the same time he admitted his homosexuality. His mother and father promptly disowned him. Then his wife took their two children and left, never to be heard of again.

Crushed by his family's negative attitude, Zane still felt the honorable thing to do was to be honest with his business associates. The board of elders quickly fired Zane as the minister of the traditional Protestant church that he had pastured for several years. No explanation was offered to Zane who held a doctorate of divinity.

To add to the piling on, Zane suddenly was "relieved" of his duties as president of the local chamber of commerce. The Lions Club International abruptly "excused" the defrocked minister as its chaplain. The county court system also notified Zane that he was no longer needed as a counselor for domestic violence cases.

All of these actions took place within two weeks of the day Zane's doctor told him of his fate.

One personal rejection devastated him more than the others. A long-planned family reunion was to take place soon at Disney World in Orlando. It was an event where he could see his mother and father, brothers and sisters, aunts and uncles, and dozens of cousins. Zane had eagerly anticipated the reunion for over a year. Suddenly members of the family balked at his planned attendance, and he was politely but firmly asked not to show up.

"It wiped me out totally," he said with emotion. "My relatives explained my expulsion was not because I have AIDS, but because I am homosexual and they don't want their children exposed to me."

"It hurt me," the thoughtful minister quietly admitted. "I decided that when I died, I didn't want these kind of relatives to come to my funeral. Since then, I have reconsidered and chosen to forgive my relatives for shunning me. You know, something good should come out of this – I mean my being forced out in sexuality and my AIDS. I have applied for the job as an AIDS program coordinator."

A month or so later I was in Zane's town judging a talent contest. He invited me to join him for dinner at his home. Walking into his living room, I felt that <u>Architectural</u> <u>Digest</u> had come to life. In the center of it all was a long dining table perfectly appointed with eighteen place settings of Baccarat crystal and Sevres china.

"Today is my birthday," Zane announced as we sat down to a one-course meal of cream of broccoli soup. "Last year ten of my friends surprised me with a lobster dinner and a birthday cake at a Jupiter restaurant." I hope that Zane didn't notice that I did not touch my soup – I was still afraid to touch much less eat food in an AIDS setting.

Rather than lie in bed all day Zane preferred to do something using his education and skills. He volunteered as a counselor at an AIDS center in Fort Lauderdale. The director said of Zane, "I don't see his kind of strength very often. I think it has a lot to do with his ministerial background. Most AIDS patients become more spiritual as they battle their disease, but he has been living a spiritual life for a long time."

When the disease sapped his energy so that he could no longer drive the hundred miles round trip daily to the Fort Lauderdale AIDS center, he reached out in another direction. He proposed a job of counseling in the West Palm Beach hospital for the terminally ill. He further proposed that when he himself was at death's door, the hospital could minister to his last needs. Oh yes, he promised all of his remaining money and wordly goods to this nationally-known hospital. Zane seemed happy and at peace with this plan.

My role as a judge and consultant on a Miss America preliminary pageant brought me again to Zane's town. My visit to my sick friend was a rather sad one. He had just received an abrupt refusal to his proposal by the hospital for the terminally ill. It appeared that their greatly publicized "death with dignity" applied to all health conditions – except AIDS.

At last the day came when Zane had to give in – he was going home to die at his unsympathetic parents. His insensitive mother and his "red neck" father were standing in Zane's front yard when I arrived. Too weak to stand, their impeccably dressed son sat beneath a white column. A moving van was backed up to the front door with four handsome, muscular guys lifting furniture inside. "I didn't know the Chippendale dancers had a moving service," I quipped to Zane. Managing a wan smile, he responded, "They are gay men from the Fort Lauderdale center who volunteered to help me move."

I faced a dilemma. At no time in our friendship had I ever touched Zane. It might have sent false signals. Also in the back of my mind, I still wondered if it were possible to contact AIDS by touching. Oh well, as we said our last goodbyes, I pressed my arms around his emaciated body and noticed the purple mark on his neck. "I want you to have my Christmas tree; please celebrate Christmas for me." And he waved goodbye.

The Christmas tree lasted the three weeks until December 25th, but Zane did not. "It was one of his last requests that you be notified of his death," his mother said in her telephone call to me hardly two weeks from Zane's moving day.

Bach, John: Chapter 14, and closing with the music of "The Lord's Prayer" was Zane's planned memorial service selections. Never in his wildest dreams did he imagine that his ravaged corpse would be paraded in an open casket for four full days before his burial in the Kentucky small town cemetery. The graveside service for the once-handsome man, barely thirty years old, was preceded by a small traditional funeral. Zane's memorial services wishes were ignored. Instead overly sentimental hymns accompanied a minister's message that "AIDS is God's punishment to homosexuals." What a funeral sermon! The only things missing in this inappropriate sermon was visions of the fires of hell and declarations of eternal damnation.

I was somewhat amazed when out of the blue Zane's mother sent me a detailed letter describing the funeral. The woman proudly included a cassette tape of the entire incredible funeral service.

Several weeks after Zane's funeral I received a late night telephone call from, of all people in the world, Zane's father. He sounded nearly hysterical. His raving and ranting appeared to be heavily laced with alcohol. When I finally managed to understand his slurred words, he was talking about some incident that occurred at the hospital the night before Zane died. It seemed that his son wanted him to read to him aloud a page from a book that was on the bedside table. The page was a description of Lady Lawford's wedding night in a book that I wrote called <u>BITCH</u>. He said he read the page to Zane; Zane smiled and then sank into his final coma.

"You Goddamn son of a bitch!" the profane father cursed me, "He smiled for you – he never smiled for me!"

SHEILAH GRAHAM

When the grand old lady of Hollywood gossip Hedda Hopper died in February 1, 1966, I placed a black wreath on the front door of my Hollywood Hills apartment. At my previously-planned dinner party that evening each guest was given a black armband and led to a table adorned with a single black velvet rose. I was crushed when I could not travel to Pennsylvania for the big-hatted gossip maven's funeral.

When the Beverly Hills funeral of gossip columnist Louella Parsons occurred on December 13, 1972, I was there. Whether she was a gracious lady or an evil bitch, the plump Louella nevertheless reigned once as "Hollywood's First Lady," ruling the film industry with her pen of vitriol.

When the third of the gossip columnist triumvirate – Sheilah Graham – died on November 18, 1989, in West Palm Beach, Florida, I was there. The presence of these three women – Hedda, Louella, and Sheilah – with their own special brand of journalism – obviously prompted me to jump head-first into gossip column-writing myself. And for more than twenty years!

Who was this dazzling blue-eyed blond Sheilah Graham, who seemed to be first discovered when writer Robert Benchley hosted her engagement party at Hollywood's famed Garden of Allah? Her fiancé was none other than the Marquess of Donegall, the wealthy British playboy. However, what of this Graham gal who claimed London birth, Paris finishing school, royal debut, and marriage to a British Army major?

At this same party Sheilah saw the novelist F. Scott Fitzgerald, and almost at first sight, they fell in love with each other. Despite Sheilah's engagement to the Marquess of Donegall and despite F. Scott's marriage to Zelda Sayre, the couple impulsively moved in together immediately.

After extended unmerciful questioning by Fitzgerald, she finally confessed her secrets. Sheilah Graham was really born Lily Sheil in Bradford, England, about 1908. Until she was fourteen years of age she lived as a charity case in the wretched East London Home for Orphans. Answering a classified advertisement "WANTED: Girls with good teeth," poor Lily erased her miserable existence by simply exposing her gorgeous smile. Yes, her toothpaste modeling at Gamage's department store soon led to her marriage to an aristocratic customer, Major John Graham Gilliam. It was he who arranged for his child bride to study acting at the Royal Academy of Dramatics Arts, and it was also he who had Sheilah presented to the King and Queen of England.

"I couldn't type or spell at all," Sheilah Graham confessed when she was hired as a journalist on the New York Mirror and the New York Evening Journal. In 1933 she left her husband behind for her writing career in New York City. Within two years the North American Newspaper Alliance offered her a Hollywood syndicated column. Eventually Sheilah wrote daily for nearly 200 newspapers – much more than her competitors, Hedda and Louella. Her $5,000 a week salary was often more than some of the movie stars that she was writing about.

Although John Wayne and Howard Hughes were serious suitors, Sheilah Graham never veered from her brilliant literary wonder boy F. Scott Fitzgerald. However, the great romance turned violent as a result of Scott's alcoholic, self-destructive behavior. Fitzgerald collapsed at her feet, dead of a heart attack. Sheilah later wrote a best-selling book Beloved Infidel about her three and one-half years with the novelist. The hugely successful book became an even more successful romance movie starring Deborah Kerr and Gregory Peck.

Since 1941 Miss Graham had been retreating almost yearly to that sunny resort called Palm Beach, Florida. So it really was no surprise when she retired from nearly forty years of gossip writing for North American Newspapers, then settled into a modest Palm Beach apartment. There she wrote books.

Fame deserts, beauty fades, money dissolves, but health can deliver the hardest blow. Two major heart attacks and two disabling hip operations made Sheilah Graham almost bedridden in her last years.

It is somewhat sad when an internationally-known celebrity is not even recognized anymore on her own block. When the November 19, 1989, edition of the Palm Beach newspaper printed the details of Sheilah Graham's death, many islanders were surprised. Some were surprised that Sheilah was eighty-four years of age. A few expressed surprise that the cause of death was congestive heart failure. However, most were surprised to discover that the famous Sheilah Graham had been living in their midst for several years.

Only a small handful of people showed up at the funeral home to say goodbye.

COBINA WRIGHT

If there were such a person as a funeral judge, he would certainly award Cobina Wright's going-away event first prize. In the beginning, a beautiful historic church – All Saints Episcopal Church in Beverly Hills – was selected for its theatrical backdrop. The excellent pipe organ and choir filled the scented air with tastefully-chosen musical compositions. The expensive color-coordinated blossoms were artfully arranged in geometric designs.

"Where is the casket?" you might ask. How gauche! Sophisticated people like Cobina Wright do not have a coffin on display – it would mar the memorial picture. After all, that's why it's called a memorial service. Cobina's service too was held at the fashionably late hour of four o'clock in the afternoon. It was perfect timing for the after-service private reception offering Beluga caviar and Dom Perignon champagne.

> Everyone who knew her is richer for her outgoing Nature, her interest in others, from presidents and royalty to those who must struggle for what they want in life.

"Who the hell is Cobina Wright?" you may be asking. Well, you obviously have not been a longtime member of Los Angeles social set. Cobina reigned for twenty-five years as the queen of society journalism for the Hearst newspapers in Los Angeles.

Born Elaine Cobb on her father's Oregon cattle ranch, she traveled to Europe in her teens to study opera. By 1916 she made her operatic singing debut at Covent Garden in London. Appearances in Paris, Vienna, Rome and other major cities soon made the new musical star the darling of European high society and royalty. In 1924 she made her American debut at Carnegie Hall. Later the strikingly attractive singer became immensely popular in the posh supper clubs. Her singing career came to an end when she began appearing in motion pictures in Hollywood.

The first husband of Cobina was Owen Johnson, author of such children's books as <u>The Varmit,</u> <u>The</u> <u>Prodigious</u> <u>Hickey,</u> and <u>Stover</u> <u>at</u> <u>Yale</u>. Divorce ended that marriage. Then she married multimillionaire socialite William May Wright. Of this union was born a daughter named Cobina Wright, Jr. Unfortunately the young girl did not inherit her mother's beauty, talent or charming personality. People found it difficult to forgive Cobina Wright's biggest flaw: she was a classic "stage mother," shoving her ill-equipped daughter to drown in deep social waters.

"B-R-E-N-D-A-A-A"

"What is it, C-O-B-I-N-A-A-A?"

The above words, delivered in ghastly nasal voices, introduced a popular parody of an imaginary telephone conversation. The two mimicked voices supposedly belonged to vain debutante Brenda Frazier and social wannabe Cobina Wright, Jr. The pair of vapid airheads became a popular fixture on the hit <u>Jack</u> <u>Benny</u> <u>Show</u> on national radio network.

In the meantime "Big" Cobina Wright was establishing herself as a social hostess extraordinaire – a role that followed her for the rest of her life. Some of her parties are legendary. Who can forget the spur-of-the-moment lavish party that she and husband William Wright gave the night of the 1929 stock market crash? They had lost four million dollars that morning.

Not long before Cobina Wright suffered that fatal stroke on Easter Sunday (April 9, 1970), I was an invited guest at one of her "salons," borrowing the name from the French gatherings. Her fame as a hostess was derived from her artful mixing of her friends from the entertainment and literary worlds with those of society and politics. As she charmingly smiled and then remarked to me that evening, "I'm not a name dropper; I just know everybody!"

On the evening that I was a guest at Cobina's beautifully decorated Beverly Hills home, the many guests enjoyed mounds of exquisite foods and the best of imported bubbly. After dinner the regal hostess called everyone into her spacious drawing room to enjoy her planned program. First, world famous health guru Gaylor Hauser spoke on "How To Live 150 Years ." However, the main speaker was actor Glenn Ford who expounded on "Reincarnation: My Last Life as a Canadian Mounty." There were not enough chairs for the guests to sit down for the speaker presentation. Since I was considerably younger than most of the guests, I offered to sit on the floor next to the fireplace. It was at least five minutes before I leaned forward and observed the slouched figure sitting cross-legged on the floor on the other side of that carved, white marble fireplace. It was Greta Garbo!

So who will attend your services? Well, Cobina Wright in death drew a full house. Gucci, Pucci, Dior, and Givenchy with loads of Cartier, Tiffany and Arpels were to be found kneeling in every pew. One glance across the crowded sanctuary quickly revealed the "A-List" personages paying tribute to Cobina. That also included Walter Pidgeon, Robert Cummings, Reginald Gardner, Robert Stack, and Cesar Romeo. Each was a close personal friend.

And will you be able to find a preacher to say complimentary words about you before dirt covers your coffin? It so happened that the distinguished minister, Dr. Gene Emmet Clark, a long-time personal friend of Cobina, delivered her eulogy:

> Everyone who knew Cobina Wright is richer for her courage, vitality, wit and gaiety. She was the perfect example of what one person can do to ease adversity with a sense of humor.

ROBERT F. KENNEDY

"My God, what a pageant!" exclaimed Lady May Lawford as she watched the Bobby Kennedy funeral with me on television. "I had no idea it would be so amusing. Will they ever get that bloody body in the ground?! Not since Jackie gave Bobby's brother such a big sendoff have I heard such clopping of horses and such beating of drums. You'd think that they were copying the Queen Elizabeth's 'Trooping of the Color.'"

"May, sometimes I think your mean-spiritedness knows no boundaries," I admonished the senior ladyship of the English colony in the United States.

"Hmmph! What does a young whippersnapper like you know about how the Kennedys have treated me. They are the rudest family in the world!" Then growing more somber, May Lawford lamented, "I wouldn't wish death on anyone's children. Nevertheless, I find the Kennedys like many redneck Irish-turned crooked Americans. Their motto seems to be: I don't know and I won't ask."

"All that they ever did to you was show a lack of respect and a lapse in good manners," I said to the internationally-known social hostess.

"Pshaw! The Kennedys and their henchmen tried to silence me, kidnap me, and deport me. Why, Old Joe Kennedy even plotted to murder me if I interfered with his son Jack's presidential campaign!

"What about your funeral train invitation?" I asked.

"I am even suspicious of *it*. The entire train trip for 1,000 people across the country from Los Angeles to New York strikes me as a gigantic political ploy. Anyway, with my arthritis acting up and my past history with the Kennedy family, it is much more comfortable watching on a television set at home." Suddenly Lady Lawford changed her conversation and lifted her glass of sherry, "Here's to Bobby Kennedy's funeral!"

"Anytime I think of Bobby Kennedy, I recall the time out at Pat and Peter Lawford's beach house in Santa Monica. There he was grown, already married, and with umpteen babies – sitting with a small table between his legs. Lady Lawford piped up, "If he had kept that table between his legs more often, his blowsy wife Ethel might not have pumped out a baby every ten minutes. And they call that *good* Catholics! Anyway…what was I talking about before you interrupted me? Oh yes, I was telling you how Bobby straddled a little table in the den armed with a knife and fork while screaming loudly like a child: 'I want my lunch! I want my lunch!' What he wanted and what he needed were two different things – he needed a swift kick firmly placed on his behind."

I remember that night in June of 1968. Studying stage and film directing under Sherman Marks at UCLA, I left my evening class on time with several of my classmates. The three strippers that I was directing in the college production of "Gypsy" loudly proclaimed, "We're hungry!" Another classmate suggested the free food at the Kennedy campaign party at the Ambassador Hotel. We were off. Once we encountered the wall-to-wall crowd at the political gathering, we searched the ballroom for the buffet tables. I am sorry to admit that we UCLA theatre students were busy feeding our faces as the assassin's shots rang out ending the life of Robert F. Kennedy.

Funeral observations by Lady Lawford and me: The Bobby Kennedy funeral event took on the appearance of a television repeat offering a flag-draped coffin followed by a black-veiled widow and an overly long ceremony…The requiem mass at New York's St. Patrick's Cathedral was conducted by Archbishop Terrence J. Cooke resplendent in conical headgear resembling a bejeweled dunce cap. Assisting was Boston's Cardinal Cushing who was trotted out at each of the Kennedy scandals. And then there was Bishop Fulton Sheen, gracing the cover of *Pulpit Daily* and a perennial candidate for Best-Dressed Clergyman of the Year… "Those are my four grandchildren sitting next to Ethel Kennedy. The same grandchildren that I am not allowed to see," said Lady Lawford, both hurt and bitter.

"What I find most interesting in Teddy Kennedy's eulogy of his dead brother," said Lady Lawford, "was Bobby's quotes about 'real love.' The slained senator and attorney general even said, 'real love is something unselfish and involves sacrifice in giving.' Ha! What does he know about sacrifice and unselfishness?"

"Well," I opined, "he might know about 'real love.'"

"Sure," Lady Lawford scoffed, "did he learn about 'real love' when he was having sex with Marilyn Monroe in the car parked in front of my son's beachhouse?! And how sacrificing and unselfish was Bobby Kennedy when he was screaming at poor, fragile Marilyn Monroe when he and Peter were at her house only hours before she was mysteriously found dead."

Lady Lawford looked off into space: "I sometimes wish that I had not spoken a word all those years ago about Jack and Bobby's affairs with Marilyn – my life might be so different today."

BARNEY PALACIOS

Imagine being a teacher in a desert resort school when one day a student simply lowered his head on his desk and never raised it again. One minute he was a seemingly healthy and happy boy playing in the schoolyard; some minutes later Barney Palacios appeared lifeless.

Thursday, April 24, 1980 - THE DESERT SUN, Palm Springs, Calif.

Sixth-graders
remember friend

Barney Palacios, age 12, died March 14 of cardiac arrest at UCLA Medical Center in Los Angeles.

The following Tuesday memorial services were held for him at Our Lady of Solitude Catholic Church. His classmates served as the honor guard.

He was a student in the sixth grade class at Katherine Finchy School taught by Beau "Buddy" Galon.

To honor Barney's memory his classmates wrote this tribute to him. It is a compilation of 30 sixth grade students' written papers. Each word was written by his classmates.

* * *

Tribute to Barney

Dear Barney,

Remember when we used to hang around the school's bike rack and talk about which bike was the best?

Remember when you asked me to go to karate class with you? Gosh, you were rather good.

Remember when I met you on the school bus for the first time? I thought you were the nicest kid I had ever met.

Remember when on Halloween night when we all went "trick or treating" on Rose Avenue? You said that you were too old for that.

Remember when we were playing football together one day? You always thought that you were not a good player, but you were just as good as the rest of us.

Remember when you dropped the ball in a bat ball game, and it cost us the game? You were not a great athlete, but a very good sport.

Remember when you brought binoculars to school and bragged about your "supervision"?

Remember when you would let me ride up and down Rose Avenue with you on your bicycle built for two?

Remember when we had chili and beans for breakfast at your house? I didn't feel so well the rest of the day.

Remember when a big boy came up and hit me on the back? You flipped him through the air. When he got up, he ran like crazy. Boy! He never pushed me around again.

Remember when I used to call you "Barney Rubble" from "The Flintstones"?

Remember when I wouldn't participate much in sports activities, and you said, "Aw, c'mon. Don't feel bad if you aren't so good at it. Play games with us."

Barney, I have never experienced death before – it is very hard for me to realize that you are gone. When I saw your casket pass by and when your mother began to speak at the memorial service, it was then I realized you were not coming back to class with us.

Why did you have to die so young? You never griped. You always looked at the good side of everything. You never did anything to hurt anyone. Who knows why God takes some of us by death sooner than others? Maybe death is God's way to let someone know that he cares about them, and doesn't want them to live in pain. Perhaps our teacher was right when he said at the funeral, "Barney may have been too good to live here – maybe God needed him more there with him."

Death is scary and also heartbreaking. When we lose someone we love, it seems like a punishment. We feel lost, empty, angry, upset, unhappy, depressed, sad – but happy because Barney, you are somewhere that is worthwhile. You will always be with us so long as we want you to be. I am sure that you will live forever in our hearts.

Yes, I feel that you are in our hearts and souls. Barney, I hope that you will watch over us as we work and play. Please be our Guardian Angel.

Barney, we will try to say a prayer for you every night. We miss you.

We all love you
The Sixth Grade Class
Katherine Finchy School
Palm Springs

KING PETER OF YUGOSLAVIA

King Peter is dead!

Long live his heir Prince Alexander!

On Tuesday, November 3, 1970, King Peter II of Yugoslavia died in a Los Angeles nursing home of pneumonia. He had been suffering many other ailments such as massive internal bleeding.

Young Prince Peter, following his father Alexander I's assassination, had been crowned king by the patriarch of the Serbian Orthodox Church back in 1941. Nine days later the newly-crowned monarch, only eleven years old, was forced to flee his country when the German army invaded and then occupied Yugoslavia.

The teenage ruler managed to escape to England where he eventually attended Cambridge University. King Peter also established a government-in-exile while residing in the United Kingdom.

In 1944 there was a complete takeover of Yugoslavia virtually making King Peter's return to native country impossible. Finally, on November 19, 1945, the Yugoslavian royal government ceased to exist, and King Peter was now out of a job.

Seriously, the truth is that King Peter's income ended when the royal government ceased to exist. "For me," he once said, "the years after the war had been a lost decade – I had gone through a fortune, but now I was penniless."

Life appeared to be one struggle after another for the former monarch. Surprisingly, King Peter wound up in Riverside, California, where he had accepted an honorary position at the Sterling Savings and Loan Bank. Within a year he left.

I first met former King Peter II when Lady May Lawford and I motored from Beverly Hills to Claremont. Lady Victoria Stevenson, a cousin of

Queen Elizabeth, was having us to tea. As we passed through the affluent village of San Merino, Lady Lawford requested that we stop at a bank there. There was ex-King Peter in a position similar to the one he held in Riverside, "Lady Lawford, would you please serve on an international advisory board?" he asked. "Why not, Pete?" retorted the outspoken aristocrat.

Controversy raised its ugly head very soon after the death of King Peter. There were those who insisted that the cause of death was suspicious. Others felt the choice of the location of the funeral was appropriate. Many Yugoslavian natives called the decision of his final resting place "ridiculous."

Despite accusations of murder, the coroner declared that the former King Peter's death was from complications from kidney failure. "Arcadia, California, is no place to have a state funeral for a man who was king," protested some family members. Yet they obviously did not understand that the deceased monarch previously chose his own church for his services.

Attorney Sam Silverstein came forth with the ex-king's last will and testament which specifically stated that the deceased had chosen the Eastern Serbian Orthodox Monastery at Libertyville, Illinois, as his final resting place.

The big day had almost arrived. To accommodate the thousands of mourners expected to pass by King Peter's coffin, the body was scheduled to lie in state at the church on Saturday, Sunday, and Monday.

However, on Saturday, November 7, church officials called off the lying in state for the exiled ruler because of threats received to steal or burn the remains. Thus, the body was hidden in "a place of safety." In the meantime, it appeared that more and more people felt that their former Yugoslavian leader should be buried in Europe.

Finally the actual 11:00 a.m. funeral service was held at the Christ the Savior Serbian Orthodox Church in the small, nondescript town of Arcadia, California. Many heads of state, members of royalty, and representatives of noble families were present. After all, King Peter was related to every crowned head of Europe. His father was the late King Alexander I of Yugoslavia; his mother was Queen Mary, formerly Princess Mary of Rumania, daughter of Queen Marie of Rumania and great-granddaughter of Queen Victoria.

I attended this funeral at the request of Lady May Lawford, who was the Senior Lady of the British Colony in the United States. She had been invited to sit in a special reserved pew just behind the former king's family. When her Ladyship was not feeling well enough to attend the funeral that day, I was pressed into service. So it was I who sat in Lady Lawford's seat directly behind King Peter's widow, Princess Alexandra of Greece, now living in Venice, Italy; his son Alexander; and the ex-monarch's two brothers.

At the conclusion of the long, dragging, and sometimes quite boring service, the family, royalty, nobility, and heads of state were led up to the altar where the corpse reposed. I hesitated at joining the others – after all, I was only representing Lady Lawford. A large man dressed in black took my arm and led me to the others.

There each of us was escorted individually to the rather ugly dark wood Egyptian-style coffin. Every one of the people ahead of me leaned over into the low casket to kiss King Peter. I had never, ever pressed my lips to a cold, clammy corpse. As I peered down at what looked like a large piece of beef jerky, I dipped down low with my back to the assembled mourners. I just could not bring myself to kiss King Peter!

Just when I thought that I successfully had control of the uncomfortable situation, a fierce-looking rabbi with a bushy black beard comes toward me. He extends to me a large silver chalice from which I am expected to drink just like the people before me. The unrecognizable black liquid tasted absolutely ghastly!

The time had come to name a new king in the event that Yugoslavia reinstates its royal government. The obvious successor was King Peter's only son Alexander. However, the young prince was out-of-sorts over the selection of his father's final resting place. He had hoped that King Peter would be laid to rest alongside his mother, Queen Marie of Rumania, at Windsor Castle in England.

Crown Prince Alexander, who was born at Claridge's Hotel and was reared in London's Buckingham Palace, was an officer in the Royal Army at the time of his father's death. When offered the Yugoslavian kingship, he declined – at least for the present. In a terse statement he said, "I am going back to my army unit. There is nothing more to say."

CASS DALEY

It was just a piece of glass. Yes, a relatively small piece of glass that ended the life of singer-comedienne Cass Daley. Was it a freak accident:? You be the judge.

Fifty-nine-year-old Cass Daley, who had been drinking the night of March 22, 1975, evidently tried to rise from the sofa in her living room. She stumbled and fell, hitting her head against the coffee table and at the same time breaking a large goblet.

Police investigation theorized that the veteran performer's neck was penetrated by a shard from the broken glass goblet. Her jugular vein was clashed. Then she got up from the floor after her fall and walked into the bathroom where she got tissue to stem the flow of blood. Finally, Miss Daley returned to the living room, lay down on the sofa and died.

About 10:45 that Saturday evening Miss Daley's husband, Robert Williamson, discovered the body when he returned home. There was a scene of blood, broken glass, and a nearly-empty bottle of vodka on the floor near the sofa. The wound was partly hidden by the pearls that she wore around her neck.

Cass Daley, whose real name was Katherine Dailey, started her show business career when she left her native Philadelphia to go across the river to Camden, New Jersey. There in a rundown bistro the skinny girl with a huge derriere was billed as a torch singer.

Her buck teeth and non-stop mugging just did not go with the torrid love songs that she sang as a nightclub performer. It was her new agent Frank Kinsella who convinced her to try comedy. The new comedienne achieved immediate success replacing Judy Canova in New York appearing in *The Zeigfeld Follies of 1936*.

Paramount Pictures in Hollywood sent for her and signed Cass Daley to a coveted seven-year contract. Soon she was appearing in such films as *Riding High, The Fleet's In, Out of This World, Star Spangled Rhythm,* and *Red Garters* in 1954.

Based on her vaudeville years, her popular radio show, and her films, Cass Daley, toward the end of her life, was attempting a comeback. Her involuntary retirement from show business for twenty-five years brought on the obvious attempt to cash in on the nostalgia craze. Los Angeles newspapers called Miss Daley's cabaret act "tried and dated." Her trademark zany comedy – grimaces and body contortions – were dismissed as "endless" and "grotesque."

I first met Cass Daley about the time that she was rehearsing for her comeback. In a seaside town called Newport Beach, some forty-five minutes south of Los Angeles, we met by accident as we walked in opposite directions on a private street in our mutual neighborhood. Yes, as I was walking down to Buddy Ebsen and John Wayne's houses to see their boats, who knew that Cass Daley lived across the street from these two stars?

For at least a year I had been appearing as the society entertainer at a very posh private club – only 500 feet from la maison de Daley. Nightly I entertained such luminaries as Shirley MacLaine, the Ronald Reagans, Julie Andrews, the Barry Goldwaters, and Joan Crawford. It truly was a rather head-turning audience.

But then came the night that a very drunk Cass Daley interrupted my performance at the exclusive club. Before I could prevent her, the middle-aged rather unattractive woman had climbed up on top of my grand piano. She next treated the curious audience to a view of her white cotton panties. Flashing her buckteeth and assuming a spread eagle position on her back, she bellowed boozily, "Play 'Melancholy Baby'!" Believe it or not! The inebriated Miss Daley sang an excellent rendition of the old ballad – before the club's security officers gently escorted the wobbly woman out the door.

"The family said no funeral is planned," reported *The Los Angeles Times* on Monday, March 14, 1975. Cass Daley's family was her husband on nine years, Robert J. Williamson, and her son, Dale Kinsella, a 27-year-old attorney by her first husband, agent Frank Kinsella.

Family minds must have changed because within forty-eight hours I was sitting in the Pierce Brothers chapel paying my respects to the late singer-comedienne. She was to be buried right across the street at the Hollywood Memorial Park. Isn't that convenient?

"She was a funny lady whose sense of humor and creative talents enlivened all who knew her" eulogized Dr. Robert Burke in melliferous tones. Sitting next to Dorothy Lamour, I remained unmoved by the tribute to a "great entertainer" until the service unexpectedly closed with a recording of Cass Daley singing "Please Don't Talk About Me When I'm Gone."

As I and the seventy-five other mourners exited the mortuary chapel after the funeral, an old dilapidated black Cadillac limousine pulled up to the curb. Judy Canova, a singer-comedienne of Cass Daley's era, hopped in followed by the psychic Criswell. Their chauffeur was a teen-age boy with orange bleached hair and robin's egg blue eye shadow.

Some time later when I was visiting that cemetery, I decided to stop by Cass Daley's resting place – someone had decorated it with a vodka bottle.

LOUELLA PARSONS

That scratch. Was I the only one to notice that large scratch across the top of gossip columnist Louella Parson's expensive bronze casket? Who could be guilty of this act of desecration and why?

I first saw the snaking indentation on the upper half of the casket at her rosary recitation on Tuesday, December 12, 1972, at 7:30 p.m. The next morning I attended the Requiem Mass for the ninety-two-year-old woman at the Church of the Good Shepherd located at 505 North Bedford Drive in Beverly Hills. Bedford Drive was especially significant to me: (1) I now lived on Bedford Drive; (2) I had a cat named Bedford; and (3) I had learned from a family genealogist that a Duke of Bedford was my ancestor.

Among the pallbearers selected for the veteran Hollywood reporter were Ronald Reagan, Gregory Peck, Bing Crosby, Jimmy Durante, George Burns, Danny Thomas, and Bob Hope. Dr. Rex Kennamer, "the doctor to the stars," was also on Louella's pallbearer list. He is the physician who discreetly hid knowledge of movie stars' abortions, alcoholism and drug use, and domestic violence from the news media. Oh yes, Miss Parsons wanted her longtime butler, Lewis Collins, to also be a pallbearer.

Freeport, Illinois, was the birthplace on August 6, 1881, of Louella Oettinger. At age ten she wrote her first story "The Flower Girl of New York." When an editor rejected it, she falsely told him that she was dying and to have it published as that was her deathbed wish. He published it, and a hint of Louella's future ethics was glimpsed.

She began her career with a five-dollar-a-week job as society editor of the Dixon, Illinois *Morning Star*. At seventeen Louella married John Parsons and had her only child Harriet. A short time later Louella is found working at the *Chicago Tribune* for $9.00 a week, and without a husband. The estranged mate John Parsons died in World War II.

Louella Parsons' life changed dramatically when she wrote a story called "Chains." The old Essanay studio paid her twenty-four dollars for the story which they made into a silent movie starring Francis X. Bushman. Coming up with the idea of writing a column about people in the movies, Louella eventually attracted the attention of publisher William Randolph Hearst. He gave her the Hollywood beat on his chain of newspapers and raised her single-digit salary to 250 dollars!

Writing the first movie column to be syndicated from Hollywood, Louella Parsons plunged into the excitement and reveled in the glamour. She came to the film capital Hollywood of the 1920s – a colorful, wacky, wonderful, mad, and exciting kind of town. It was the time of Clara Bow, Tom Mix, Gloria Swanson, Douglas Fairbanks, Norma Talmadge, Mary Pickford, and Rudolph Valentino.

Many people say powerful Louella ran Hollywood, but more accurately Parsons typified what Hollywood was. She made it important, and it, in turn, made her important.

Hedda Hopper, Louella's greatest nemesis, and Hollywood writer Adela Rogers St. Johns were able to tell about Louella Parson's more colorful side. For example, it was thought that the publisher William Randolph Hearst gave Louella her high-paying columnist job to keep her quiet about the mysterious death of director Thomas Ince on Hearst's yacht. The volatile, ballistic, vengeful nature of Louella reaped gifts from the people she trashed in print: a box of rotten eggs, a rattlesnake in her mailbox, and a package containing a live skunk.

Mrs. Hopper, the tall blonde stylish actress-wife of the distinguished actor De Wolfe Hopper, was Louella's opposite. Hedda was always fashionably dressed with a trademark hat; Louella was short, dumpy and her taste in clothes was dowdy. Hedda's voice was cultured; Louella's resembled a screeching peahen. Hedda could spell and possess writing skills; Louella had better keep her job with Hearst!

On the set of a movie called *The Oscar*, about Frank Sinatra, a feisty Hedda Hopper told me the best Louella Parsons story that I ever heard. It concerned Louella's second husband, Dr. Harry (Doc) Martin, a notorious venereal disease physician, who now worked at the studio – thanks to his wife. One evening Louella and her husband were engaged in their usual partying, when suddenly the alcoholic doctor passed out and lay on the floor.

"Can I help him to the sofa?" asked the host.

"No, no, don't disturb Doc," said Louella, "he has to perform surgery at seven o'clock in the morning!"

Toward the end of Louella's life I tagged along with the editor of Hollywood's first fan magazine (Photoplay), Adela Rogers St. Johns, on her visit to Louella. The gossip columnist was in her eighties by then and living in the Berkeley East Convalescent Home in Santa Monica where she died. Her diagnosis was "generalized arterial sclerosis."

When Adela and I entered Louella's bedroom, she was sitting close to the television and talking to the screen. It was apparent to me that the show she was watching was the soap opera, *All My Children*. Every so often Mrs. Parsons would say to the woman on the screen, "Oh, Mary, you look so lovely," and to the man on the screen she swooned, "Oh Doug, you are the best swashbuckler." When the couple kissed on the television show, Louella clapped her chubby hands and exclaimed, "My wonderful Mary and Doug – they're back together again!" Puzzled, I questioned Louella's longtime acquaintance Adela about the seemingly bizarre behavior when we left the nursing home. Adela explained that Louella evidently was having delusions that the soap opera actors were Mary Pickford and Douglas Fairbanks whose divorce in 1927 was one of Louella Parson's biggest stories.

Upon ninety-two-year-old Louella Parsons' death, the Hearst newspapers unleashed its "hearts and flowers" journalism division. Result: Calling Louella "First Lady of Hollywood" in the headlines. A fifty-year-old picture of Louella smiled from above the newspaper banner on front page. Was the deceased really the "evil bitch" or "black widow spider" or Hollywood's "gracious lady?"

Louella lived and breathed Hollywood, worked and played with it, praised and scolded, encouraged its strivings and pointed out its weaknesses, rejoiced and sorrowed with it!

Goodbye, Lollipop

MORTON DOWNEY

One sunny afternoon in the early 1980s regular patrons of Palm Beach's only supermarket, Publix, were suddenly distracted from their selections of caviar and champagne. Loud voices shattered the usual peace and serenity of the upscale grocery store. The disturbing noise seemed to be coming from Aisle 9 where the macaroni and spaghetti products were located. There stood two men vociferously and boisterously disagreeing on the other's choice of pasta to be purchased for the evening meal. Had Publix customers looked closely they might have recognized one of the men as local resident Morton Downey, once the singing rage of America. The other man? Oh, that was Downey's dear friend and frequent houseguest, Frank Sinatra!

Sean Morton Downey was born in Wallingford, Connecticut, the son of a tavernkeeper. By the time that he was eighteen, he was vocalist with the famous Paul Whiteman Orchestra. By 1926 show business impresario Florenz Ziegfeld had stolen Morton Downey away from the Whiteman band to appear in his South Florida production *Palm Beach Nights*. It was from this time on that the Irish singer sought out a life in high society.

After establishing himself as an international star, Downey returned to New York City to open his own supper club called the Delmonico. Now he reigned as the singing prince of New York's café society; but that was not enough – it was not high society.

Syncopation was the first motion picture that Downey made after going to Hollywood in 1929. In the movie he sang the hit song "I'll Always Be In Love With You" to his co-star Barbara Bennett. By the completion of this firm the two stars married. Downey's new father-in-law was the patriarch of the famous acting family – Richard Bennett – whose other two daughters were actresses Constance and Joan Bennett.

While Downey was becoming a multimillionaire through his many entertainment endeavors, his personal life was in tatters. His alcoholic wife left him for a little-known movie cowboy named Addison Randall, leaving behind five children. Eventually, Barbara Bennett committed suicide.

In 1950 Morton Downey remarried. This time the "Irish Thrust" wed an heiress from the Biddle family of Philadelphia named Margaret Boyce Schulze. Called "Peggy," Morton's new wife was considered one of the richest women in America. Peggy had gained a reputation as a fun-loving socialite during her marriage to Prince Alexander Hohenlohe. Later, Hohenlohe lived out his life in the Palm Beach area with his new wife, the irrepressible entertainer Honeychile Wilder. Always a devout Catholic, Downey fought long and hard to have the Catholic Church annul Peggy's first marriage to Prince Hohenlohe. Finally awarded the annulment, Morton and Peggy were then wed in a religious ceremony. In their fourteenth year of marriage, Peggy died after surgery for breast cancer. A mob of Palm Beachers greatly mourned the loss of one of the most popular women on the Palm Beach social scene.

Morton Downey had two best friends and the two close friendships endured over a considerable number of years. Joseph P. Kennedy and the popular vocalist knew each other socially because of Irish and Catholic bonds. However, they became bosom buddies when Kennedy shared the secret that he had his daughter Rosemary lobotomized without even telling his wife Rose Kennedy. Downey also gave permission for doctors to perform one of the first prefrontal lobotomies on his daughter Lorelle, a gifted athlete. As far back as 1926 when Kennedy hosted movie screenings at his rented Clarke Avenue home in Palm Beach, Morton Downey was on a permanent guest list. When Jack and Jacqueline Kennedy married, the Irish balladeer sang at the wedding reception. Downey even loaned his Cape Cod home to Kennedy's son, President John F. Kennedy, which in 1962 was used as the summer White House. For fifty years at virtually every major gathering of the Kennedy family, Downey would sing the requested "Sweet Adeline" while Rose Kennedy loudly sang along in a shrill soprano voice.

The other dear friend of Downey's was Frank Sinatra. Perhaps it was only natural that there would be a close friendship between the best-known Irish crooner and the best-known Italian crooner. Year after year they remained close. How close were they? Well, when Sinatra married his fourth wife Barbara Blakeley Marx in a top secret 1976 wedding, he honeymooned at Morton Downey's home with Downey present.

For a man who aggressively sought to be in high society, Morton Downey may have unconsciously sabotaged his own social aspirations. His close friendships with Joseph P. Kennedy and Frank Sinatra, both men of questionable connections, easily prevented Downey from being totally accepted by Old Guard society or "A" List social circles.

When Downey married for the third time, he chose attractive widow Ann Van Gerbig whose golfer son wed Victoria Fairbanks, daughter of actor Douglas Fairbanks. Even with wealth and fame, Morton Downey seemed forever doomed to café society rather than high society. Ironically, his new wife moved freely in the highest social circles while designing the interiors of their mansions.

Late Friday evening, October 25, 1985, the eight-three-year-old Morton Downey died at his 601 Island Drive mansion in Palm Beach. The entertainer who had appeared in Command Performances before President Franklin D. Roosevelt, King George, Queen Elizabeth, and the Prince of Wales now had come to his final performance.

A ho-hum, less than inspiring funeral mass took place the following Monday at noon at St. Edward's Catholic Church in Palm Beach.

Frank Sinatra and wife Barbara flew in for the funeral. Some members of the Kennedy family attended. However, conspicuously absent were members of high society.

LEO G. CARROLL

"Hey!" was the loud voice that shattered the silence. "Hey, young man, what are you doing?"

"I was only picking a lemon," I protested hesitantly.

The scene was a beautiful California morning in 1965 when I dashed out of my Hollywood Hills apartment to pick a lemon for my tea. I was on the back terrace reaching up over the edge plucking a lemon from the branch of a neighboring tree.

"Oh, very well, young man, take all of the lemons that you wish. I have plenty," said the man with the booming voice.

"Thank you, sir," I mumbled quietly.

Seldom have I felt so ill at ease as at this very moment. For, you see, I was totally naked except for a skimpy red speedo swimsuit while the distinguished gentleman was nattily attired in English tweeds.

One day later my landlady explained that the "gentleman" who had caught me stealing a lemon was our next-door neighbor, the venerable English actor, Leo G. Carroll!

How exciting it was to live next door to a real live movie star! I had enjoyed him in such movies as "Spellbound," "Waterloo Bridge," "Wuthering Heights," "Rebecca," "The Snows of Kilimanjaro," and "The Bad and the Beautiful." He had appeared in literally dozens of films.

Of course, Leo G. Carroll became a household name when he starred in the title role of "Topper," the television series. Later he gained an enormous following playing Mr. Waverly in television's "The Man From U.N.C.L.E."

Born in Weedon, England, Carroll debuted on the London stage in "The Prisoner of Zenda" in 1911. After his honorable discharge from a British infantry regiment, he made his acting mark on Broadway starring in such plays as "Angel Street" and "The Late George Appley." Scores of motion pictures and television followed.

The very proper character actor always greeted me in the mornings when we both went to our cars. However, it was a mutual friend who transformed us from being just neighbors into close friends. That friend, author Patrick Mahony, gave wonderful dinner parties on one Saturday evening a month. Regular guests for dinner included Pola Negri, Anna Lee and Robert Nathan, Countess Tolstoy, Gloria Swanson, and Queen Mother Elizabeth of Belgium. Both Leo G. Carroll and I were on that coveted guest list.

It was slightly ironic that Carroll's charming wife Edith Nancy was a patient at Hollywood Presbyterian Hospital when her husband died there at age 80. Her hospitalization prevented her from attending his funeral the morning of October 19, 1972 at Blessed Sacrament Church, down the hill from our Whitley Terrace residences.

PETER DUEL

There sprawled naked beneath a Christmas tree was the dead body of actor Peter Duel. A gun lay nearby.

Thirty-one-year-old Duel, co-star with Ben Murphy in the television show *Alias Smith and Jones*, evidently shot himself in the head – at least that is what both the police and coroner investigation concluded.

Diane Ray, Peter Duel's longtime girlfriend, retired for the evening at the Hollywood Hills home the two shared. He stayed up watching a basketball game. Miss Ray said that Peter came into their bedroom about 1:25 a.m., taking a gun, saying "I'll see you later."

Bang! A shot rang out that was heard by Miss Ray, and she rushed into the living room where she saw him nude, tangled in the Christmas lights under the tree.

It was New Year's Eve of 1971.

When the police saw the gun at Peter Duel's feet, they assumed that it was a suicide in which two bullets had been fired. However, it was determined that the actor had fired one shot the previous month in anger upon receiving a telegram notifying him that he had not been elected to the board of the Screen Actors Guild. Thus, he lost the opportunity to be among the likes of such illustrious SAG members as Ronald Reagan, Patty Duke, and Charlston Heston.

Diane Ray, 29, told investigators that earlier Thursday evening she and Duel had watched his television series *Alias Smith and Jones*, and then they discussed his despondency over his drinking problem. Only last June he was place on probation for felony drunken driving after pleading guilty.

Born the son of a doctor in Rochester, New York, Peter Duel (real last name: Deuel) studied medicine at St. Laurence University. Switching to acting training in New York's American Theatre Wing, he succumbed to Hollywood's beckoning for a recurring role in the television series *Gidget.*

I first met Peter Duel at the preview of his first television series *Love on a Rooftop.* He and co-star Judy Carne (later Burt Reynolds' abused wife) were such friendly, fresh-faced newcomers eager to please the Hollywood industry guests.

When next I ran into the handsome actor, he was grubby in appearance and seemed to be quite inebriated. The occasion was an appearance by his beloved sister Pamela singing at Ye Little Club. Ye Little Club, an intimate neighborhood nightspot in Beverly Hills, was my favorite handout. On its tiny stage appeared three of my favorite performers: Vicki Carr, Jack Jones, and Joan Rivers.

"Peter Duel's spirit is now free from the body and has risen and rests in the bosom of God," said Guru Dhamandanda at the January 2 memorial services held at the Self-Realization Fellowship in Pacific Palisades. This serene setting with its formal gardens had formerly belonged to the murdered actress Thelma Todd – so said my funeral partner Thelma Keaton who had been "Hot Toddy's" partner in film and frolic. Anytime that I attended any funeral services with filmland fixture Thelma Keaton I was always late. This memorial service for Peter was no different – we were so late that we could not join the 120 relatives and friends seated in the chapel. Instead, we were part of the 200 people standing outside the chapel listening to the Hindu scriptures over the public address system. So much for being irreplaceable in the Hollywood film industry:

Filming on the Universal Studies' set of *Alias Smith and Jones* closed down for four hours on the morning of the popular TV star's death. In the afternoon, studio auditions were held in hopes of finding a replacement for Peter Duel in the series by the next day.

PRINCE ALEXANDER HOHENLOHE

Funerals of royalty or nobility can be quite boring. Although the corpse and the cast of characters may be colorful, the actual ceremony of death may prove to be very tedious. Uninspired music, monotonous ministers or priests or rabbis, inappropriate casket, and lackluster flowers can all contribute to the ruin of the final memorial picture.

Prince Alexander Hohenlohe, 65, was visiting his daughter Catherine Jacobus at her Delray Beach, Florida, home when on January 9 he died of a heart attack. About fifty people attended the funeral services three days later at St. Vincent Catholic Church in Delray Beach, Florida.

Prince Hohenlohe, a descendant from Austrian and Polish nobility, was related to the Hapsburgs, the ruling family of Austria and Hungary. He was also a distant cousin of Prince Philip, husband of Queen Elizabeth II of England.

Formally known as Princess Alexander Hohenlohe, the tall, slender widow looked unaccustomed to her conservative black garb at the funeral. Most people seemed to know that the widow was the flamboyant woman who changed the life of the Austrian prince.

Patricia Wilder, the widow's maiden name, left a Georgia farm behind at age 16 and took New York by storm. Within one day of her arrival in the Big Apple, the southern belle had been hired as a showgirl and appeared that night on the Bob Hope Show at the Palace Theatre. She became a regular on his radio show while appearing in a dozen forgettable Hollywood movies.

Quickly becoming the darling of New York's café society, Miss Wilder could be found day and night at the "21" Club, the Colony, the Café Pierre, El Morocco, and the Stork Club. She became known on this social circuit as the dark-haired beauty who called everybody "Honeychile." In turn, she herself found that she soon came to be called Honeychile herself.

Honeychile Wilder never denied her affinity for millionaires and celebrities when she considered romance. After the end of her celebrated engagement to King Farouk of Egypt, she had close relationships with publisher Conde Nast, composer George Gershwin, columnist Walter Winchell, and even J. Edgar Hoover. It was author Truman Capote who used Honeychile as the prototype of his heroine Holy Golightly in his work *Breakfast At Tiffany's*.

Headlines all over America screamed "Showgirl Marries Prince" and "Meet Princess Honeychile" when Alexander and Patricia wed. Thus began a union of his nobility and title and her special brand of electricity.

After their marriage, the couple accomplished a momentous feat: they managed to unite nobility with international society with café society. They turned their fifteenth-century castle, Schloss Mittersill, into a private resort club situated in the Austrian Alps. Lovely Honeychile's ingenuity, candor, and contacts combined with Alexander's lineage guaranteed an abundance of American heiresses and European blue-bloods.

Schloss Mittersell included among its membership: The Duke and Duchess of Windsor, William Randolph Hearst, Henry Ford, Anheuser Busch, Bob Hope, and Prince Kumar of Baroda. Prince Alexander Hohenlohe had an extremely handsome first cousin named Prince Alfie von Auersperg. One day on the grounds of the mountain resort, Alexander introduced Alfie to the beautiful heiress Sunny Crawford. Marriage followed and the birth of Alexander and Ala. Sunny's second husband was Claus von Bulow.

Prince Alexander and Princes Honeychile, aside from Schloss Mittersell, maintained residences in Palm Beach, New York, and Marbella, Spain.

Standing on the steps of the church after the funeral service was the son of the deceased. His name is Christian Alfred Hohenlohe, and he is the treasurer of the Smithsonian Institute.

THE MYSTERY CORPSE

Would the real mystery corpse please stand up – or – lay down? Is it Arthur Halverson? Is it Andrea Freeman? Is it David King?

As people entered the slumber rooms of Palm Beach Memorial Park Funeral Home, they first stepped gingerly into a room with a female corpse. Could that be the person that they had come to pay respects to? Or was it the deceased man in a casket in the next slumber room? Which person's visitation had caused people to wolf down their supper, put on a tie or heels, and drive across town in rush-hour traffic? Yes, it was indeed the Mystery Corpse.

A male baby was born January 31, 1937, in Milwaukee, Wisconsin. He was named Arthur Halverson. Arthur established himself as a versatile athlete in his local community. By high school, the tall, muscular young man with Nordic features realized that he did not want girls – he wanted to be a girl!

After a high school graduation, Arthur joined the Navy where he sampled sex with the prostitutes while stationed in the Philippines. Over the next eight years he did more than merely sample sex with some young ladies – he married three of the young ladies. By age 29 Arthur had been divorced three times, and had fathered three daughters.

By now Arthur Halverson had entered show business. As an entertainer appearing in nightclubs, he billed himself as Art Mann and the Mann Act. Later he adopted the name Erik North, appearing as "the modern Viking of song."

1971 was a breakthrough year. This was the year that Arthur or Art or Erik took stunning singer Cheryl Edwards as his fourth bride. She traveled the world with him adding her beauty and her talent to the musical act. The couple's sexual relations were good. However, the multi-married husband and father's growing urge to become a woman now seemed irrepressible.

"I am not gay," he said flatly. The man also denied that he was a transvestite, deriving sexual gratification from feminine clothing. As the 600 dollar-an-hour entertainer told a <u>Palm</u> <u>Beach</u> <u>Post</u> reporter: "I never disliked myself as a man. I was a fun guy. I loved the person that I was. But I hated my penis."

So Arthur Halverson a.k.a. Art Mann a.k.a. Erik North chose to surrender his manhood. In 1980 the sex reassignment surgery took place in Colorado. Of course, the actual surgery was preceded by the required preparatory steps recommended by experts of gender reassignment. This included living as a woman for a year and regular psychiatric sessions during this time. Cosmetically speaking, he had been taking hormones and had grown breasts; painful electrolysis was employed to get rid of unwanted hair. At last the forty-three year old man emerged from the Colorado clinic a woman named ANDREA.

Ooops! The newly-assembled Andrea needed to return to the repair shop. Her brand new private parts needed cosmetic surgery to pretty them up. Rhinoplasty gave Andrea a smaller and more feminine nose. All the while the freshly-made woman endured more and more electrolysis to make her hirsute body and thick beard a distant memory.

Her first job after achieving womanhood was as a private secretary in Atlanta. Fortunately she went relatively unnoticed. However, Andrea yearned for a higher-profiled life: she craved again the spotlight as an entertainer.

Night after night she sang in a sultry voice and did a comedy act in various nightclubs. With her slinky sequin evening gowns revealing very ample décolletage, with her long showgirl length blonde hair and with her long, long slender gams peeking through the seductive slits in her skirts – Andrea was quite striking.

Still, the nightclub singer chose not to tell her audiences about her transgender surgery. People wondered about her six foot, three-inch height; the broad shoulders and large hands drew gasps; and there were whispers about the strange voice. All the time smiling Andrea kept mum about her secret. Is it a "he" or a "she"? The mystery actually may have added to the entertainer's professional mystique.

(I interrupt Andrea's transgendered tales to tell you of an evening back in the early 1970s at a Beverly Hills nightclub called Por Favor. I was having dinner with the internationally-famous male-turned-female Christine Jorgenson. While we were eating our dinner, a very obvious transgendered female swept by our table. Whereas Christine looked at me smiling and said, "And to think that I started all of this in Denmark in 1950!)

Love came to Andrea unexpectedly. After being a nervous groom four times previously, she at last became a blushing bride at age fifty-two. She married sixty-one year old retired businessman Arthur Freeman, moving to his Lake Worth, Florida, home. After the death of the well-to-do cancer-stricken widower seven years later, Andrea confessed that she had never told her late husband that she was a transsexual.

Can you guess what happened next in our hero's – er –heroine's unpredictable life? Well, let's see. It took Arthur Halverson forty-three years to become Andrea while ripping his body and family apart by even daring to marry a man. Now after being a woman for eighteen years, Andrea wants to be a guy again! Reversal surgery and all. No wonder The National Enquirer found this story irresistible!

Enter Wife Number Four once again. Gorgeous songstress Cheryl Edwards had been forced to walk away from the ten-year marriage when her husband attempted to solve his gender confusion with a scalpel. Ignoring her ex-husband's eighteen years as Andrea and blotting out Andrea's marriage to businessman Arthur Freeman, Cheryl proved to be extremely forgiving. She professed that she still loved her ex-husband, and her ex-husband confessed that she had always been the love of his life.

David King, a biblical name, was the spiritual appellation that Andrea chose when she began the transformation from woman back to man. However, the road to manhood had its obstacles – David wanted to have Andrea's D cup breasts greatly reduced, but that surgery takes lots of money. Can you imagine the thousands and thousands of dollars that it would require to reinstate David's male genitalia? So for a while the newly-christened Mr. David King would have to live as a man rather than be a man.

Once again Cheryl Edwards and Arthur Halverson/Art Mann/Erik North/Andrea Freeman/David King were together again – as partners in life and in their dual careers. The very pretty and curvaceous Cheryl and the rather feminine David revived their musical act appearing in local country clubs and condominium activity centers. This time David poked fun with his audiences about The National Enquirer's picture of him in pink lace lingerie and high heels.

As I entered the small chapel at Friday noon, March 1, 2002, the funeral of David King was about to begin. At the front by the casket were three dark-clad rear ends mooning not only me but also the other thirteen people sitting in the pews. The display of derrieres was three adults (one, the minister) bending over to the floor where there was an uncooperative sound system that resisted their efforts. How very fitting for an entertainer with a broken life to have a broken p.a. system at his last gig!

For a brief moment the Palm Beach Memorial Park Funeral Home in Lantana, Florida, seemed to come to life. Some of the deceased's children and eight grandchildren presented music, and the minister spoke about David King's "mistake."

On a lush living room sofa in front of the casket (the rest of us were seated on hard wooden pews) sat the most attractive widow clutching the wedding band that the corpse gave her thirty years ago.

THE MANSON MURDERS

Sharon Tate and Jay Sebring

"Don't go to get a haircut today – I don't know why. It's something in your chart" was the message on my telephone answering machine from my astrology teacher Maureen Dragone.

I didn't see Maureen often, and we seldom talked on the telephone, so how did the well-known astrologist know that I did have an appointment at my hair stylist on that day?

"That day" was August 8, 1969, and my hair appointment was for 5:30 p.m. – about seven hours before the most brutal massacre ever to occur on the west coast. It was a tragedy that sent shivers throughout the entire world. The bloody victims of both savage stabbing and senseless shooting included actress Sharon Tate, my hair stylist Jay Sebring, coffee heiress Abigail Folger, playboy Voyteck Frykowsky, and the young hitchhiker guest of the caretaker, Steven Parent.

10050 Ciclo Drive, a lonely estate at the top of Beverly Hills, had once been the home of actor Cary Grant and his wife, actress Betsy Drake. Later, the secluded redwood house was the love nest for record executive Terry Melchoir, Doris Day's son, and his live-in love, actress Candice Bergen. Finally, this same estate was now the leased home of Polish director Roman Polanski and his wife actress Sharon Tate. This was the scene of the orgy of killing, the impulsively sadistic mass murder of five innocent people.

I really did not know Sharon Tate well on Wednesday, August 13, when I attended her funeral. Since the Hollywood movie colony is fairly close-knit, I had seen her on occasion and we had spoken. Miss Tate was a very pretty woman in a town of pretty women. I had seen her in the movie

<u>Valley</u> <u>of</u> <u>the</u> <u>Dolls</u> in which her role as a naive film sex symbol was over-shadowed by veteran actresses.

At Sharon Tate's morning funeral service at the chapel atop the steep incline at the Holy Cross Cemetery at Culver City, I have never cared for this cemetery: the hillside is too steep and the nearby freeway is too noisy. Still, it does boast the unique downhill water cascade marking showman Al Jolson's memorial.

Kirk Douglas, Stuart Whitman, Warren Beatty, James Coburn, Peter Sellers, and Yul Brynner were among the many members of the Hollywood movie colony who heard the Rev. Peter O'Reilly of Good Shepherd eulogize her: "She was a fine person, and we were in no small measure devoted to her."

The mourners, already filled with terror and fear for their own lives, shuddered as they stared at Sharon Tate's silver-colored metal casket. Only four days before the beautiful blonde actress was stabbed sixteen times while trying to protect her unborn child and begging, "I want to live. I want to have my baby!"

I never liked Polish film director Roman Polanski. Maybe it was his matted brown hair that looked unclean. When he married Sharon Tate, I wondered if she knew of his track record with women. Whispers in my neighborhood for quite some time had Polanski connected to the wild sex and drugs. Thus it was no real surprise when Roman Polanski was deported for the drugging and raping of a thirteen-year-old girl, with his friends Angelica Huston and Jack Nicholson lurking in the background.

While Polanski leaned over to kiss the casket in a farewell to his twenty-six-year-old wife, the funeral director handed Sharon's mother five pink roses from the large spray of roses on the casket. When asked about the absence of Mass, Father O'Reilly said, "The family wanted only a brief ceremony." Many of the mourners were upset that their flowers were piled on the lawn in front of the chapel. The explanation offered by the funeral attendant was the 150 people present crowded out the floral arrangements. Two tall pedestal-mounted bouquets of marguerites flanked each end of the caskets – actor James Coburn used strong-arm tactics to get his flower arrangements placed in the chapel.

* * *

In 1969 I was working at The Symposium of Beverly Hills located at 9212 Wilshire Boulevard. Upstairs offices were occupied by former California governor "Pat" Brown with visits by his son, Jerry Brown, future state governor. In the small office to the left of my office was a couple that I said only "hello" and "goodbye" to. I had trouble pronouncing his Polish name correctly, and I only knew her as "Gibby."

Imagine my amazement when I picked up the morning edition of The Los Angeles Times and saw a picture of the guy with the hard-to-pronounce name and also the woman called Gibby. They were the house guests at the Tate-Polanski residence that awful night of slaughter.

Voyteck Frykowski was found lying about twenty feet from the front door. His face and head were totally crushed in; his stomach, chest, limbs, and back had fifty-one stab marks, thirteen club marks and two gun shots. The jet-set playboy's girlfriend, Abigail (Gibby) Folger, was also murdered by multiple stab wounds. She was the Radcliffe-educated heiress to the Folger coffee fortune.

* * *

More than four years before the so-called Manson murders, I went with a friend to get his haircut in a luxury shop located in West Hollywood. As I sat in the beautifully decorated lobby, I thought that I recognized at least two men sitting there – George Hamilton and Ryan O'Neal – waiting to have their haircut.

When my friend had finished getting his haircut, his hair stylist Jay Sebring came out and was introduced to me. "Any friend of Jerry's is a friend of mine," said Mr. Sebring, reaching up to feel my hair. "Oh, virgin hair and your own natural blonde color – let's see what we can do for you." At the end of thirty minutes the creative hair stylist worked his magic making my hair truly a work of art.

"You seem vaguely familiar to me," I said to Sebring." "Wait a minute! Do you know James Clutter of Bessemer, Alabama?"

He smiled, "I am James Clutter of Bessemer, Alabama!"

Flabbergasted, I gasped, "Then you used to cut my hair when I visited my cousin Bruce who lived on the same street as your barber shop."

"Yes," said Sebring, "I left all of that behind when I came to Hollywood to become an actor."

We shook hands and exchanged pleasantries when all of a sudden I remembered that I had not paid for my haircut.

"Your hair styling is thirty-six dollars," said Jay matter of factly.

"Eeeeck!" I screeched. "What happened to those one-dollar haircuts you gave in Bessmer?"

"Oh, okay. Since you are a struggling actor from back home, I'll let you off for twelve dollars," said Jay, "But for this discount I expect you to model your hair in my hair shows."

Thus began the business relationship and friendship between the celebrity hair stylist Jay Sebring and me. No, we were never really close. I would usually book his last appointment of the day for a hair styling once a month. He would ask me everything about the current stage play that I was appearing in when we went out to a nearby bistro after my hair cutting. Once he took me over to entertainment reporter Rona Barrett's place – she had been his girlfriend in drama classes. He talked to me again and again about his heart's desire to be an actor. Yes, I knew that he kept marijuana and cocaine in the door pocket of the driver's side of his foreign sports car. We never mentioned the subject of drugs.

On August 8, 1969, I was late in making my appointment for hair styling with Jay. He told me to come on in anyway – he would make me his last customer of the day. He also asked me if I wanted to go with him afterwards and meet a good friend. He didn't say who, but I agreed readily. When I called Jay later that day, I explained that I was stuck in a play rehearsal and must cancel my appointment. I wondered who the "friend" was that I did not get to meet...

We now know that Jay Sebring, after closing his salon that night, went to 10050 Ciclo Drive to visit actress Sharon Tate. At one time Jay had been engaged to Sharon. Now he was very good friends with both her and her husband Roman Polanski who was away on film location. Jay was, as always, stylishly dressed – white tailored pants, blue striped shirt with black leather belt and boots.

Hours later Jay Sebring would be found in the living room. He had been both shot and stabbed many times all over his body. A bloody towel was wrapped around his head as a hood and a rope was knotted around his throat. The rope that was around Sebring's was also wrapped around Sharon's neck. Thrown over an exposed roof beam, the rope evidently was meant to hang the two victims. The baby was ripped from Sharon's stomach and Jay's dismembered penis was crammed into her mouth!

Barely two hours after Sharon Tate's funeral, many of the same film stars rushed to the nondenominational services for Jay Sebring. At the Wee Kirk o' the Heather, the same quaint church where Will Rogers and Jean Harlow had funerals, was an overflow crowd. Hair dressers were in great evidence. Also many of Sebring's customers who had become his close friends such as Steve McQueen (he recently had Jay fly to an Ireland movie location for a $2500 haircut). Henry Fonda, Peter Fonda, Paul Newman, Alex Cord, and George Hamilton populated the large sorrowing group.

Beautifully coiffed Steve McQueen stumbled through a brief eulogy. He was followed by a friend, Alvin Greenwald, who eulogized Sebring as "an individual human person who earned and deserved the trust and respect of us all."

Many of the men and women wept openly by the time that they were ushered from the flower-bedecked chapel. Singer Keely Smith sobbed convulsively. Director Roman Polanski, who came direct from wife Sharon Tate's graveside, was so shaken that he had to be supported by friends on each side.

Because of his Bessemer, Alabama, father's insistence, Jay Sebring's funeral featured an open casket. At the end of the service everyone was routed to the casket where the body of our friend reposed. Ahead of me gossip maven Rona Barrett audibly gasped when viewing the body. Just in front of me in the line was George Hamilton; on viewing Jay he leaned back so far on his heels I though that he might topple onto me. Then it was my turn to view Jay: Oh, my gosh! Rope burns were still visible on his jawline and on his neck; stab marks peeked out from his shirt collar; and some yucky green mucous was oozing out from a wound in his neck. Even the excellent cosmetic department of Forest Lawn Memorial Park could not hide the signs of the savage murder.

Outside of the Wee Kirk o' the Heather chapel I was talking to George Hamilton. Both Paul Newman and Steve McQueen were standing with us, occasionally contributing a comment. A National Broadcasting Company (NBC) cameraman came up to us and asked permission to film. McQueen, Newman, and Hamilton removed their dark glasses and patted their hair, preparing for the filming. Of course, I moved out of camera range – I realized that I am not a movie star!

"I'm sorry. I only want the guy in the white suit," said the cameraman pointing at me.

"Me?" I asked timidly.

"Yes, you. Your white suit and blonde hair will give color contrast to the background people…Now over here…fall to your knees and slowly lift your hands in prayer…that's good…stay in that position while I bring in the cross on top of the chapel behind you…Thank you very much."

All during this filming Paul Newman, Steve McQueen, and George Hamilton stood there watching me curiously.

* * *

"You bastard! You dirty bastard!" were the words coming out of my telephone receiver. I immediately recognized the deep, rich and resonant voice of my best friend, actor Richard Brian.

"Wadda you mean?" I asked him defensively.

"Have you no shame?" he retorted. "There you were on the six o'clock news today using a funeral to get publicity."

I then explained the events of the day at Sharon Tate's and Jay Sebring's services to Richard.

Later that evening I watched the funeral sequence that was repeated on the eleven o'clock news. I cringed as I watched myself kneeling in front of the chapel's cross, my eyes lifted toward heaven.

All in all it had been quite a special day.

JACK BENNY

After parking my automobile the required distance, I began walking with the crowd to the chapel for the comedian Jack Benny's funeral service. Suddenly I accidentally bumped into a man. Not just any man – it was actor Gregory Peck.

Sheer terror registered in Gregory Peck's eyes. Did he think that I was a stalker? Or a hit man? I must confess that Peck is my all-time favorite actor for his stirring portrayal of Atticus Finch in <u>To Kill A Mockingbird</u>, but I wouldn't purposely bump into the Oscar winner.

Then what caused such horror in the face of Peck when I was accidentally pushed against him? Maybe, just maybe it could have been our own last encounter of an intimate kind. No, no, what I mean is that perennial Hollywood starlet Thelma Keaton and I were in line with Gregory Peck at the Academy Awards office. Mrs. Keaton's little dog Tweedle-dee evidently thought Peck's leg was a fire hydrant. You get the picture, don't you?

Once inside the Sunday noon service at the chapel at Hillside Memorial Park, I was aghast at the virtual who's who of Hollywood present. Leaving the Jack Benny residence together and arriving <u>en masse</u> at the funeral were the comedian's manager Irving Fein, Edie Goetz (daughter of M-G-M boss Louis B. Mayer), Sylvia Fine and Danny Kaye, Jack Lemmon, Nancy and Ronald Reagan, Delores and Bob Hope, Frank Sinatra, Rosalind Russell, and more. Rabbi Edgar Magnin officiated, and both Bob Hope and George Burns delivered eulogies.

Jack Benny was born Benjamin Kubelsky in Chicago although he called Waukegan, Illinois, his hometown. The date was February 14, 1894. As a child prodigy playing the violin in vaudeville, young Jack seemed destined to a very brief show business career so he added "talk" (comedy).

He bounced around vaudeville with his fiddle and jokes until he finally appeared in several Earl Carroll and Schubert musicals on Broadway. Then vaudeville died.

His movies came next. Starting with Hollywood Revue of 1929, Benny made numerous motion pictures such as The Horn Blows at Midnight, George Washington Slept Here, Broadway Melody of 1936, and Charley's Aunt.

Jack Benny achieved his breakthrough – starring on a radio show – after a 1932 appearance on the Ed Sullivan show. Soon The Jack Benny Show became and remained one of the most popular series on radio. For seventeen years the comedian enjoyed unparalleled success.

He next jumped ship from radio to television taking with him his wonderful cast: Mary Livingston (actually his wife Sadye Marks whom he married forty-seven years earlier); announcer Don Wilson; Irish tenor Dennis Day; gravel-throated Eddie Rochester; and bandleader Phil Harris. For the next twenty-four years the Jack Benny Show rode the crest of television's highest wave of popularity.

With a career that spanned fifty-three years Jack Benny persuaded millions of people that perhaps he was only 39-years-old (again and again) and that the old Maxwell parked in front of his house (he lived next door to Lucille Ball) was a sign of his eternal stinginess. Of course, not so many people knew that Benny had raised millions of dollars to help the poor and underprivileged.

It was in mid-December that cancer was found to have ravaged his body. Jack Benny was not told of his immediate death sentence – he thought he had a pinched nerve – so he went on planning upcoming appearances and projects. Doctors did not think the violinist-comedian would last until Christmas Day. He hung on until noon of the next day...

And then with a perfect pregnant pause and a masterful double-take, Jack Benny put down his violin for the last time.

SUSAN HAYWARD

When my paternal grandmother died, my father asked me to fly to Atlanta, then drive to Carrollton to play the organ music for her funeral. Because of lack of family closeness, I never really knew the lady. The only thing that I remembered about her appearance was her ruby stud earrings. "Where are her ruby earrings?" I asked as I looked at the shriveled-up corpse in the casket. Funeral director H.G. Hightower produced the earrings from his pants pocket.

Later I visit Mr. Hightower at his funeral home for family information when I happened to hear that his mortuary was to handle the body of Susan Hayward.

It seemed rather ironic that the flame-haired Miss Hayward and I only lived a few blocks from each other in Beverly Hills, California. When she died in her sleep at this home from a malignant brain tumor on March 4, 1975, her body was shipped to Carrollton, Georgia, for burial. As chance would have it, we would both travel nearly 3,000 miles to tiny Carrollton – she as a corpse and me as a mourner.

Born Edythe Marrener in Brooklyn, New York, on June 30, 1919, Susan Hayward first attracted attention as a hat model. When producer David O. Selznick saw Susan's photographs in the *Saturday Evening Post*, he offered her a Hollywood screen test.

Although she was beautiful and possessed considerable acting ability, Susan appeared in eighteen films before she achieved stardom. Her role as a female alcoholic in *Smash-up*, and her role as a naïve college girl in *My Foolish Heart* both won her nominations for awards by the Academy of Motion Picture Arts and Sciences.

By 1953 the Hollywood Foreign Press had named Susan Hayward "the most popular film star in the world." The same year *Photoplay* magazine recognized her stardom by naming her "the most popular actress on the screen." Both Metero-Goldwyn-Mayer and Twentieth Century-Fox studios owe their income to Miss Hayward and her remarkable film popularity.

For many years I had been a devout fan of Susan Hayward. That glorious mane of red hair and that special way in which she played vixens really appealed to me. It's difficult to select my favorite Hayward characterizations. Still, I loved her dramatic roles in *With A Song In My Heart, Back Street, I'll Cry Tomorrow*, and her award-winning *I Want To Live*.

One day in the 1960s I accompanied my father to a Carrollton, Georgia, automobile dealership. As we were looking at the new and used Cadillacs, we were warmly greeted by the owner-dealer Eaton Chalkley. It just so happened that Mr. Chalkley and my father had been college classmates. Up in the showroom was Mr. Chalkley's wife – a pasty-face woman with red hair that had four-inch dark roots. An out-dated black crepe dress covered her slender body, and a cigarette dangled from her top lip. I was shocked to find that this woman was movie star Susan Hayward.

Who would have thought that a glamorous Academy Award-winning actress would fall in love and marry a small town automobile dealer back in 1957? Yes, the star of more than fifty films wed Eaton Chalkley and left the Hollywood glamour behind for the rolling hills of Georgia. Soon she was living a simple country life, often driving into Carrollton in a pickup truck to buy groceries, wearing dungarees and a bandana covering her famous flaming tresses.

On the day of Susan Hayward's funeral, I wanted to arrive early at the church. My relatives were absolutely no help in giving me directions, but they did think that the church was out on Temple Road, miles and miles out of Atlanta.

Driving along rural Temple Road, I came upon what easily must be the most magnificent barn in the state of Georgia. The Chalkleys' barn reportedly held bulls worth $15,000 each in these luxurious quarters. Still, there was no one at the barn to direct me to the location of the church.

Traveling farther down the country road, I stopped at the only sign of life – a man standing in front of a general store. "Do you know where Susan Hayward lives?" I asked him. "You mean Writer Hayearth?" (I guess that he meant Rita Hayworth.) Anyway, changing my line of questioning, I asked, "Where is the Catholic Churth?" which brought instant directions.

At Our Lady of Perpetual Help Catholic Church – the church that Chalkleys' money built – Rev. Thomas Brew and the Rev. Danny McGuire celebrated the final rites of the fifty-five-year-old movie siren. The casket, the flowers and the music program did not reflect the funeral of a famous person. Susan's twin sons, Timothy and Gregory, by her previous marriage to actor Jess Barker, survived their mother.

Under drizzling rain Susan Hayward was laid to rest next to her loving husband Eaton Chalkley, who died in 1966. The gravesites are in the small rural churchyard that was marked by a statue of the Virgin Mary. The white marble statue was selected by the couple when they were vacationing in Italy.

BEN JOHNSON

The dark-haired, good-looking man picked up the tanned, hard-bodied roofer at a local bar by promising him cocaine. When they ran out of coke, the young stranger was ready to leave the older guy's home. However, his host reappeared wearing only a woman's blond wig, metal clamps on both nipples, and a tiny strip of leather tied around his penis. A whip and a set of handcuffs completed the sadomasochistic ensemble. In the bedroom sexual seduction was rebuffed when the younger guy punched his host and refused to remove the handcuffs. Panicking, the older man ran through a second-floor glass door and leaped from a balcony. Awakened neighbors and the police found the handsome homeowner totally naked, bruised, bleeding, still handcuffed with a fractured arm and with the would-be male sex partner standing by.

A pornographic movie? No, just another sexual encounter in the everyday life of Ben Johnson. It might have gone unnoticed if Johnson had not been married to Palm Beach socialite Ancky Revson.

It all started some sixty or so years ago when Ben Johnson was born in Blue Springs, a small town outside Dallas, Texas. He often joked that his childhood was so poor that his only toy was an old mayonnaise jar.

A good-looking face, a sculptured physique, and an adventuresome attitude led Ben Johnson into a career in male modeling. That would be the ticket that would catapult him from modest beginnings to a life of opulent wealth and jet set socializing. The door opened to him in the person of Johanna Catharina Christina de Knecht, a Dutch fashion model always called "Ancky," who had just received a fifteen million dollar divorce settlement from cosmetics tycoon Charles Revson.

Is the story true that Ancky, still flashing the thirteen-carat diamond ring that Revson had given her, was in the Colony bar in Palm Beach when she first met Ben Johnson in 1964? Evidently the fiftyish divorcee was attracted to the handsome male model from Texas who supposedly was twenty-nine years old. Thus, began a whirlwind romance that took them to Monte Carlo, London, and the Bahamas because both Ancky and Ben loved to gamble. Of course, everything was paid for with Ancky's money since Ben had no visible source of income. Finally, on June 19, 1966, in Las Vegas, Nevada, they married near their beloved gambling casinos where most Palm Beachers had actually believed they met. The newlyweds settled down in Ancky's luxurious Manhattan apartment and adopted two children – a girl named Alexandra and a boy named Douglas. After a visit to the Palm Beach home of glamorous socialite Anne Hamilton and her actor-son George and interior designer-son Bill, Ancky and Ben Johnson decided to move from New York to Palm Beach. Thus, began a procession of two adults, two adopted children, five dogs, three cats, three birds, and two monkeys.

When Ancky and Ben debuted on the Palm Beach social scene in 1974, the imposing couple injected new life into the succession of never-ending parties and interminable charity balls. Ancky, so tall and stately in her gowns that were smothered by her long ropes of pearls, and Ben, so tanned and dashing in everything that he wore, were indeed a striking couple at the island's sparkling events. That year the Hamilton brothers, George and Bill, helped Ben Johnson get into the lucrative real estate business in Palm Beach. Ben was a "natural" for this type of career, and over the years he has gained respect for his abilities. Perhaps the John Lennon-Yoko Ono mansion was his most famous sale. However, it is to his credit that he has been selected Realtor of the Year as well as President of the Palm Beach Board of Realtors.

Ben's choice of sex partners could not have been worse: each of the three young men that he was arrested for propositioning was a policeman. Ancky previously had turned her head and pretended not to know her husband's sexual secrets. Finally, a sensational divorce trial resulted in October of 1985.

Regal Ancky, resplendent always in her trademark turban, could forgive Ben's exorbitant spending; his gambling, drinking and drugging; his sexual exploits, and even his demand for alimony. However, she could not forgive him for telling the court that she was seventy-five years old!

Though divorced, Ben and Ancky remained each other's best friend. When Ancky was dying some time later, it was Ben who remained at her bedside.

Even after being diagnosed with cancer himself, Ben did not lose his sense of humor or his zest for living. He could still be seen racing his moped or tooling around town in his Rolls Royce. Not content to sit still and bemoan his fate, Johnson took off on a long, last vacation in Yemen. Who else would go to the little-known Arab kingdom of southwestern Arabia? And when at last chemotherapy caused him to go bald, Johnson covered his head with a big, black Rastafarian wig. He laughed louder than anyone.

As death approached, Ben Johnson called his adored children – Alexandra of New York City and Nicholas of Washington, D.C. – to his bedside. He instructed them not to give him a funeral or memorial service because he didn't want people to sit around mourning him. Instead, he made them promise to say that he had left town to go on his next great adventure.

When Johnson died on that October day at Good Samaritan Medical Center after a lengthy battle with cancer, the children kept their word. They bought a full-page memorial in the <u>Palm</u> <u>Beach</u> <u>Daily</u> <u>News</u> featuring a large photograph of the dashing Ben Johnson, smiling broadly, doing a dance with a straw hat and a cane.

The caption: On October 22, 1999, Ben R. Johnson left Palm Beach on his next great adventure.

His family and friends wish him well and sent him off with love.

IRENE RYAN

Comedienne Irene Ryan, the sometimes zany but always loveable "Granny" in *The Beverly Hillbillies* television series, died April 26, 1973. She was 70 years of age. The actress had suffered a stroke on the Broadway stage while appearing in *Pippin* in March. Her condition steadily worsened until her death at St. John's Hospital in Santa Monica.

Known to millions as the pipe-smoking and moonshine-making ball of energy called "Granny," Irene Ryan reigned as the matriarch of the television Clampett clan during the nine years of filming and the ongoing years of reruns.

"She had paid her dues" was the show business jargon used to express that Ryan's success was long overdue. Few people remember that in the early days of radio she appeared with her husband, Timothy Ryan, in the comedy show, *Tim and Irene*. Does anyone recall that Tim and Irene Ryan were the toast of Broadway in the 1930s? Most people seem to have even forgotten that Irene Ryan won a "Tony" award for her role in *Pippin* just before her death – forty years after she first conquered Broadway.

The diminutive actress left no heirs at her death so the millions of dollars that she left will go to the Irene Ryan Foundation. This foundation provides scholarships for theatre arts students.

It seemed that every funeral that I attended in the chapel of Gates, Kingsley and Gates Mortuary, 1925 Arizona Avenue in Santa Monica, was Religious Science. It appears that the average person is not very familiar with this spiritual belief.

"The church of the stars," the Church of Religious Science, was founded by Ernest Holmes in the living room of Pickfair, Mary Pickford and Douglas Fairbanks' Beverly Hills estate. Of the denomination of 200,000 members, probably more Hollywood stars and show people are in its membership than any other church. When I would attend regular services at the Church of Religious Science, I saw among the congregation Esther Williams, Fernando Lamas, Phyllis Diller, Robert Young, Gloria Swanson, Ann Miller, Peggy Lee, Mickey Rooney, and former child star June Withers just to name a few. Also the cast members of television shows "The Jeffersons," "Sanford and Son," and "The Beverly Hillbillies" were present in large numbers.

As the 2:30 p.m. memorial service for actress Irene Ryan came to an end that Tuesday, it closed in a Religious Science tradition. Yes, I joined hands with Bob Hope and Buddy Ebsen and sang at the top of my voice "Let There Be Peace On Earth."

EDWARD G. ROBINSON

"Life for me began when I was 10 years old," said Emanuel Goldenberg as he saw the Statue of Liberty upon arrival from his native Bucharest, Romania in 1903.

While studying law at New York City College and Columbia University, the young man won a scholarship to the American Academy of Dramatic Art. It was "goodbye law" and "hello acting." The passionate performer then changed his name to Edward G. Robinson – "a name I had heard while sitting in the balcony of the Criterion Theatre."

After appearing in forty Broadway plays, Robinson arrived in Hollywood to act in the film *The Hole in the Wall*. However, in 1931 he shook the cinematic world by its roots with his "tough guy" portrayal in the movie *Little Caesar*. This proved to be the role of his life, and the film is immortalized as a classic.

The actor's Al Capone-like role in *Little Caesar* spawned a myriad of impersonators, who as brazen gangsters, constantly snarled, "All right, you guys..."

Edward G. Robinson had already appeared in 100 films (such as *Double Indemnity, Tampico, All My Sons,* and *A Woman In Love*) by the time I first met him in 1969. One of my neighbors in the Hollywood Hills, the redoubtable character actress Beulah Bondi, took me with her to an art exhibit. What I did not know was that both Miss Bondi and Mr. Robinson, mutual admirers of each other's acting excellence, were also directors of the Los Angeles Art Association.

That evening Robinson was a very charming host. He brought me a glass of champagne, and then the esteemed actor even attempted to increase my appreciation of art. Not a chance! The art was definitely modern featuring an eye in the stomach area and an ear next to a big toe.

Nevertheless, he treated my disinterest with total civility. In fact, later in the evening he noticed that I was engaged in lengthy conversation with former matinee idol Rod La Rocque. He enthusiastically joined in.

Edward G. Robinson died January 26, 1973. He succumbed to cancer while undergoing tests at Mount Sinai Hospital in Hollywood. The 79-year-old actor, philanthropist, and art connoisseur was to have received an honorary Academy Award in eight weeks.

"One of the most gracious, gentle men I've ever known – a true Renaissance man," Robinson's friend Charlton Heston said in his eulogy in front of 500 star-studded mourners at Hollywood's Temple Israel. The "tough actor" was survived by his second wife, dress designer Jane Arden. The motion picture industry was well represented among the pallbearers: Jack Warner, Hal Wallis, and Mervyn LeRoy. His friend George Burns was named too.

The day of the Edward G. Robinson funeral I was in bed with influenza, but I went anyway. At the end of the service I vainly decided to hide my runny nose, watery eyes, and pallid complexion from the horde of movie greats. Picking up a piece of convenient cardboard, I covered my face and began pushing quickly through the crowd. Singer Lori Lane, swathed in fur, had become almost airborne while holding on to my arm. "Who is he? Is that Ryan O'Neal?" shouted the paparazzi as I literally ran from the unruly pack of photographers and reporters. In the dash I brushed up against Rosalind Russell, and I collided with comedian Groucho Marx's wheelchair. Members of the pursuing media shouted obscenities at me as Lori and I jumped into my Rolls Royce and sped away.

PRINCE ALEXIS OBOLENSKY

Chinchilla, mink, silver fox, sheared beaver, lynx, and ermine adorned the shoulders of many of the women attending. The men attending arrived in their toys – Rolls Royces, Bentleys, Jaguars, and even Ferraris and Lamborghinis. What fashionable cocktail party lured the smart set with an invitation requesting their presence on Tuesday, February 18, 1986, at 4:00 p.m.? No, no, not a cocktail party. This affluent crowd was attending the memorial service for Prince Alexis Obolensky at Bethesda-by-the-Sea Episcopal Church in Palm Beach, Florida

Prince Alexis Obolensky, always known to his friends as "Obie," had died at age 71 at his New York City apartment on February 8, 1986. The prince has been a longtime resident of Palm Beach.

Obie Obolensky's love for the game of backgammon will long make him remembered. In fact, he was eventually dubbed "the king of the game." The prince learned the game when he was a seven-year-old child from a gardener. That was just after his family of White Russian noblemen fled from Russia to Turkey. Obelensky went on to raise the board game to an art form.

After many years of lackluster interest in the game, Obie Obelensky single-handedly started the whole resurgence of backgammon, and all the real official rules. He actually started the backgammon tournaments all over the world, including some world championship events. In n1968 Obie, the man who made backgammon a household word, published a book that came to be recognized as the "Bible of Backgammon."

Living in Hollywood during the 1970s, I was well aware of the influence of Obelensky and backgammon on the movie community. Once at a West Hollywood private club called Bumbles, I witnessed a heated backgammon game with singer-actress Diana Ross, a very vocal player.

Later up the street at The Factory, the exclusive discotheque, I saw English actor Peter Lawford bent over his backgammon board. When I visited comedienne Lucille Ball to discuss a film we were making together, no sooner had she opened the door to her house she then asked me, "Do you play backgammon?"

Next to backgammon, Prince Alexis Obolensky loved Russian cooking. Were you ever invited to a dinner party at his Palm Beach home or his New York apartment? Friends raved about the Russian food feast.

Obolensky's interest in Russian cuisine was so strong that at the time of his death he was planning to associate himself with a Russian restaurant. He was going to be host – he put together the decorations, designed the menus and the clothing of the waiters, and, of course, he was overseeing the food preparation. Ironically the Petrouska Russian Restaurant, located at East 86th Street in New York, opened the very night that Obie died.

At Obie's memorial service I sat beside international society columnist Martha Cuneo Reed, also known as Princess Kaprotkin. Her presence was arresting considering her electric blue outfit – with matching lipstick, eye shadow and veil! I spoke to the deceased's two daughters Mary and Anne, and his son, Prince Alexis Obolensky, Jr. after the service. Oh, and I was also able to speak briefly with Obie's sister, Princess Serge Troubetskoy.

Wherever he is today, Obie would surely be pleased that his son, "Little Obie," and his wife Selene are keeping the tradition of annually celebrating their Russian heritage.

Prince Alexis Obolensky, Jr. and his wife each sponsor the imperial ball for about 300 bejeweled and betuxedoed guests at the Mayflower Hotel ballroom. The prince wears a costume that consists of a gold brocade tunic featuring an embroidered double-eagle motif. His princess wears a gold brocade costume trimmed with fur from the town of the prince's mother. It is topped with a jewel headdress.

The young prince, often plagued by whispers of illegal drug use and homosexuality, has turned the family's magnificent palace in St. Petersburg, Russia, into a school for orphans.

MRS. MICKEY ROONEY
(THE FIFTH)

Picture this: Four small children kicking the damp clumps of dirt at the freshly-covered grave of their murdered mother. Kelly Ann, Kerry Yule, Michael Kyle, and Kimmy Sue Rooney, all under six years of age, reacted differently to the scene of burial at the new Forest Lawn Cemetery of Hollywood Hills. The children's emotions ran the gamut from uncontrollable tears to what resembled shellshock.

For pint-size movie star Mickey Rooney, his first wife was beautiful actress Ava Gardner. His second wife was beauty contest winner Betty Jane Rase. His third wife was pretty actress Martha Vickers. Wife number four was pin-up girl Elaine Mahnken.

Then Barbara Ann Thomason became the fifth Mrs. Mickey Rooney. The English-bred blue-eyed blonde met the world famous actor at the popular Santa Monica nightclub, The Horn. It was the Hollywood version of love at first sight: Rooney said, "You're the most beautiful woman I've ever seen!" and Miss Thomason realized that here was a man who could get her into movies.

For many years the top box office champion of motion pictures, Mickey Rooney made an immediate gesture of unwedded bliss to Barbara Ann – he left his last wife. Ignoring divorce and marriage conventions, Mickey and Barbara Ann set up a household together and quickly started family plans. From 1959 to 1963 they had one child almost every year – Kelly Ann, Kerry Yule, Michael Kyle and Kimmy Sue.

While he was busy acting in such films as *Breakfast at Tiffany's* and *Requiem for a Heavyweight*, Rooney continued his wild lifestyle of alcoholic drinking and an addiction to barbiturates. He even had several sexual affairs with other women while with the always-pregnant Barbara Ann.

However, what Mickey Rooney never anticipated was that his wife Barbara Ann was cheating on him. While Rooney was in Beirut making the film *24 Hours to Kill*, his wife moved would-be actor Milo Milocevic into the marital bedroom. Barbara Ann's new lover was everything that her actor-husband wasn't – tall, dark, muscular, and very handsome.

It was just a matter of time before this explosive situation detonated. One day the Los Angeles Police Department found Milo Milocevic's body slumped over Barbara Ann's body in the master bathroom. Both had fatal gunshots to their heads, with a .38 revolver lying on the floor.

The four small children fortunately did not see their mother's naked body with her brains blown out. Apparently they were asleep in their beds in another wing of the house during the horrible incident. Fortunately they never even heard the gunshots.

The official police report stated that the deaths were murder-suicide although public opinion suspected Mickey Rooney. The Yugoslavian consul general in Los Angeles wanted to charge Mickey with double homicide on behalf of Milocevic's family, but the evidence was insufficient.

Mickey was on the arm of Marge Lane at his wife's funeral. Marge, by the way, was Barbara Ann Rooney's best friend who was with her only a few hours before her death. Everyone was caught off guard when Mickey married Marge Lane almost immediately. Living in an alcohol-drug induced state for the one-hundred-day marriage to Marge Lane, Mickey confessed that he does not recall a single day of their marriage.

Rooney's seventh wife, Carolyn Hackett, is said to resemble his slained wife while wife number eight Jan Chamberlain is considered by many people to be a dead ringer for the murdered Barbara Ann Rooney.

MAMA CASS ELLIOT

A ham sandwich. A common ham sandwich. Who would have believed a person could choke to death on an ordinary ham sandwich?

Personal physician Dr. Anthony Greenburg said in a press conference that his patient probably choked to death on a ham sandwich.

It was on Monday, July 29, 1974, that secretary Dot MacLeon found singer "Mama" Cass Elliott's body slightly propped up in her double bed. The television set was on, and a ham sandwich and a soft drink were beside her pillow.

Miss Elliott's body was discovered in her six-room luxury apartment on historical Curzon Street in the fashionable Mayfair district of London, England.

Although Mama Cass' private doctor said that her death "was the result of choking on a sandwich while in bed and inhaling her own vomit," an autopsy performed by British top pathologists found the cause of death to be inconclusive.

It was thirty-three years ago that Ellen Naomi Cohen was born in Baltimore, Maryland. When she headed for New York at age nineteen determined to have a stage career, she took as her professional name "Cassandra Elliott."

Dr. Goldberg now issued a statement saying that Miss Elliott "was a very big lady." Thus, he felt that a heart attack may have been the cause of death.

In the early 1960s the singer rose to fame as the leading Mama of the musical group. The Mamas and the Papas. They soared to music stardom with such hits as "Monday, Monday" and "California Dreamin'." When the singing group, consisting of Cass, Michelle Gilliam Phillips, her then-husband John Phillips, and Denny Doherty, broke up in 1968, Miss Elliott launched a career as a solo singer. His records featuring her sweet voice sold like the proverbial hot cakes. Her appearances at Caesar's Palace in Las Vegas reportedly earned her $40,000 a night.

Further testing from the death inquest in London determined that dieting might figure in the cause of death of Cass Elliott. "Mama" Cass was five feet, five inches tall, and she weighed 238 pounds. A doctor who treated her stepped forward to say that she had been dieting and that "had been doing quite well at it." A reporter from the *Times of London* newspaper stated that only a few days before death she had claimed to have recently lost eighty pounds.

Only two days before her sudden death, Mama Cass had closed after a two-week engagement at London's famed Palladium. She was delighted at the standing ovations, according to the singer's rotund manager Allan Carr (It was humorously suggested that they exchanged clothes.) "This last week was the happiest I have ever seen her," said Carr. She was excited about beginning a British tour of singing engagements. Immediately after, she planned to rush to Baltimore where her seven-year-old daughter, Vanessa, whose father was singer James R. Hendricks, was being cared for by her grandmother.

Dr. Anthony Greenburg, although not based on medical evidence, continued to state that he felt Miss Cass had died from choking.

Mama Cass' body was flown home to Los Angeles four days after her death. Groman Mortuaries handled the funeral arrangements. A rather generic funeral took place at 10:00 a.m. that Friday morning (with a somewhat sleepy-looking crowd) at the chapel at Hollywood Memorial Park cemetery. Being Jewish, the singer was entombed at the adjacent Beth Olam Cemetery

At the funeral I sat in a small pew in the back of the chapel. On my left side sat flame-haired comedienne Carol Burnett, in a pair of high-heeled sandals that revealed toes awry. She whispered to me: "I just loved her, didn't you?"

Rushing in late and sitting on the other side of me was Michelle Phillips, a former member of the singing group, The Mamas and Papas. I was impressed with the fresh beauty of Ms. Phillips, especially since I was familiar with her devil-may-care lifestyle.

New medical evidence reportedly revealed that Mama Cass Elliott did not choke on a ham sandwich. She did not suffer a heart attack brought on by obesity. The singer evidently did not die from the side effects of dieting. Her cause of death: an overdose of heroin.

MOLLY WILMOT

She was the consummate Palm Beach socialite. Yes, she did committee work, charity galas, and dinner parties. As a typical social figure, she served as committee member, chairwoman or honorary chairwoman for many fundraisers such as the American Cancer Society's Palm Beach Benefit, the Hospital Ball, the April In Ball in New York, and the Saratoga Hospital benefit auction.

The "she" is the personable and pretty Molly Wilmot, the socialite who divided her life between her homes in Palm Beach, Florida; Saratoga Springs, New York; and New York City.

Older and less attractive social matrons might criticize her short, short skirts or her deep cleavage. However, could that be because they did not look as good as she? In her years Molly Wilmot paraded around at parties in figure-hugging "cat suits" that revealed her traffic-stopping curves.

The Palm Beach Post listed Mrs. Wilmot's age at death as 78. The Palm Beach Daily News reported that she died in New York on Wednesday, September 18, 2002, at age 73. Molly's sense of humor would surely have seen the irony in the age discrepancy.

The Mass of the Resurrection was held at 10:30 a.m. the next Tuesday, September 24 at St. Edward's Catholic Church in Palm Beach, Florida. Frank E. Campbell and Son Funeral Home in New York was in charge of funeral arrangements. By the way, at the Palm Beach memorial service I sat in Pew 13. That was the pew in which Colonel Edward Bradley always sat. You remember him, don't you? The ill-gotten gains from his illegal gambling business financed the church.

Mrs. Wilmot was born Mollie Netcher on May 9 to Charles and Gladys Oliver Netcher in Chicago, Illinois. Young Mollie graduated from the Foxcroft School. However, since their father was head of a multimillion dollar Midwestern department store chain, Mollie and her sister spent their younger years bouncing back and forth between Los Angeles and New York.

Husbands – the blonde heiress had three: Eddie Bragno, Albert Bostwick and Paul Wilmot. When she married publicist Paul Wilmot at her home in December of 1970, none other than society queen Mary Sanford served as her matron of honor. Later, after the Wilmot divorce was final, someone asked Mollie if she had picked her next husband. The three-time divorcee is reputed to have said, "My next husband hasn't been born yet!"

Now Mollie Wilmot took time out from her world travels and philanthropic work for The National Museum of Dance and the New York City Ballet to establish permanent residency in Palm Beach. She selected the 1075 North Ocean Boulevard house that was built back in 1941 for pharmaceutical heiress Evangeline Johnson, then Princess Evangeline Zalstem Zalesky. Mollie's biggest complaint that first winter was the large number of Secret Service men roaming her property while assigned to her neighbor President John F. Kennedy.

On the night of November 23, 1984, the relatively low-key socialite went to bed anticipating the photo shooting the next day by <u>Town and Country</u> magazine of her pool area. After all, her poolside cabana was considered beautiful and her swimming pool was one of the largest on the island.

"Ma'am, it is your regular 9:30 morning wake-up time and here's your breakfast tray," said Mollie Wilmot's maid that next morning. "But first, ma'am, won't you come see this boat that washed up in the night?"

"No, I would rather have my breakfast. After all, small sailboats are always washing up on the beach."

Finally giving in to the insistent urging of her maid, Mollie put on her robe and walked into her living room. The tanker beached next to her swimming pool was so large that the stunned socialite couldn't see the ocean or the palm trees through her windows. The ship's bow was resting just a few feet from her living room.

"When I saw it, I was speechless," Mrs. Wilmot said of first seeing the freighter. "You cannot imagine what it's like."

The rusted freighter was actually a 197-foot Venezuelan vessel named the Mercedes I which soon became known as "Molly's Mercedes."

Ever the perfect hostess, Mollie Wilmot is said to have come aboard the tanker, bearing champagne and caviar, to greet the captain. Moreover, she asked her servants to give fresh-ground coffee and food to the crew who were ordered by the Immigration and Naturalization Service to remain aboard the ship.

By now, helicopters were flying overhead, and the Palm Beach police were directing the hordes of sightseers stopping at the Wilmot home next to the Kennedy compound. Suddenly there were literally droves of media camping out on her grounds.

Donning vanilla-colored clothes to match her vanilla-colored hair, Mollie Wilmot went out to meet the press. Armed with martinis for all, Mollie's charm, graciousness, patience, and good humor fast made her the darling of the newspapers and television. Soon all of America recognized this smiling woman wearing large cream-colored designer sunglasses, holding her tiny dog Fluff, standing in front of the rusted Venezuelan freighter.

One day Mollie Wilmot was just another Palm Beach socialite; overnight she became a national celebrity. Unrelenting public attention continued to follow her. Even Disney studies wanted to make a movie called <u>Palm Beached</u> with Bette Midler playing Mollie. Mrs. Wilmot said "no" to the project that promised to be a zany comedy lacking dignity and respect.

At Mollie's memorial mass many mourners seemed unaware of Mollie's serious role as a horse breeder. Hence, her home in Saratoga Springs. She asked that contributions be made in her memory to equine research at the Veterinary College of Cornell University.

On March 6, 1985, the 660-ton houseguest named Mercedes I was finally towed away after 105 days wedged next to the Wilmot swimming pool. In the words of Mollie herself: "Obviously, it was the most monumental thing that ever happened to me, having an incredible happening like this come into your life. The Mercedes will always be the winter of '85 in my life."

ARMAND HAMMER

Armand Hammer, the oil billionaire often accused of being a Communist, planned his bar mitzvah for December 11, 1990. Of course, this ceremony is for a Jewish boy, thirteen years old, reaching the age of responsibility. However, ninety-two-year-old Hammer insisted on the much-delayed celebration – even if it was seventy-nine years late. Doing things in his usual manner, Armand Hammer planned for 800 invited guests, each were required to donate $500.00 to Jewish charities. The only problem was that Hammer was late again to his bar mitzvah. You see, he died just hours before the celebration.

Although it has often been stated that he was Russian-born, Armand Hammer was actually born in New York City on May 21, 1898. His parents, Julius Hammer and Rose Lipshitz were Jewish immigrants from Russia.

Armand's business acumen was already apparent when he was an undergraduate in medical studies at Columbia University. Taking tincture of ginger, he made and sold delicious ginger ale. He made his first million dollars with the drink, and he wasn't even twenty-one years old yet.

Leaving behind his Socialist father, who help found the American Communist Party in 1919, the medical school graduate decided to live in Russia. Immediately all Soviet doors were open to him. Young Armand Hammer suspiciously parlayed meetings with Soviet leader Lenin in Moscow into a vast personal fortune, a business empire providing American grain for Russia, and a lasting major role in international affairs.

Adultery is a word that might be used to describe the romance pattern of Armand Hammer. He first fell in love with Baroness Olga von Root, a glamorous singer who was married. Impetuously they ran away together finally marrying two years later. The baroness hated their exclusive residences in Moscow, Paris, and New York, but loved their Palm Beach winter place. Little did she realize that her husband was chasing actress Helen Hayes and painter Frances Tolman. When the Hammers divorced, Olga named Angela Carey Zevely as "the other woman." Sure enough, only a few days later, Angela became the second Mrs. Armand Hammer. History repeats itself: before the ink could dry on the divorce papers from Angela, Armand married his now-attached love, painter Frances Tolman.

Absolutely ruthless and without ethics, Hammer reveled in the fact that he had immediate and unlimited access to heads of state unmatched even by the president of the United States. He even bragged about how he could drop in unannounced on Prince Charles and Princess Diana.

A shameless self-promoter, an outrageous egomaniac, and a publicity-mad media manipulator, Armand Hammer traveled with cameramen, photographers, and reporters. They were not the ordinary media – they were all people hired by him to give him the appearance of being a newsworthy celebrity.

I stood outside the relatively new Armand Hammer Museum of Art in West Los Angeles looking through the windows. Inside the museum were the 800 invited guests who had originally planned to attend Hammer's bar mitzvah. The gathering, which occurred on December 11, 1990, became a tribute to Hammer's life. He was eulogized as a crusader for world peace and a remarkable philanthropist at this most unusual funeral-memorial service.

When the big tribute had ended, many of the 800 guests literally poured into the street. I rushed ahead of them across Wilshire Boulevard, up Glendon Avenue, to Westwood Memorial Park. Ostentatiously overpowering the graves of all of the movie stars was this grandiose pink mausoleum near the entrance of the cemetery. Engraved in gold across the top was "The Armand Hammer Family" where the new sarcophagus reposed. Although Armand Hammer may have been the most influential private citizen of twentieth-century America, he would not have been very happy – you see, many of his mourners were ignoring his resting place and were gathered at the nearby grave of Marilyn Monroe!

JEANETTE MACDONALD AND NELSON EDDY

Jeanette MacDonald is remembered as "gracious, feminine, and very friendly" while Nelson Eddy is recalled as "warm, sensitive, humorous and happy"…"both are gone now but they will never be forgotten – their music will live forever." These were the words of America's premier tap dancer Eleanor Powell who worked with them in the golden reign of Metro-Goldwyn-Mayer movie studio.

The funeral of Jeanette MacDonald on January 18, 1965, was my first big Hollywood burial extravaganza. Also, it marked my second visit to Forest Lawn Memorial Park in Glendale, California – probably the most deluxe cemetery grounds in America.

As I drove my convertible into the Forest Lawn entrance at nearly two o'clock in the afternoon, I was again impressed by the lush greenery and the impressive statues. Arriving in the vicinity of the Church of the Recessional, I was awestruck at the size of the crowd who had purportedly come to pay respects to their singing diva. Actor-husband Gene Raymond had kindly provided loudspeakers so that the many friends and fans who could not get into the church could hear the service.

One look at the printed funeral program and you knew that you were witnessing a real Hollywood event. The list of honorary pallbearers included former Presidents Eisenhower, Truman, and Nixon, and Chief Justice of the Supreme Court Earl Warren. Sitting down front were future President Ronald Reagan and Senators Barry Goldwater and George Murphy. Glimpsed in the funeral crowd were Jeanette MacDonald's former singer partner Nelson Eddy, director Alfred Hitchcock, and such film personalities as Spencer Tracy, Irene Dunne, Allan Jones, Greer

Garson, Lew Ayres, Jane Powell, Buddy Ebsen, Jack Oakie, Johnny Mack Brown, Mary Pickford with husband Buddy Rogers.

Actor Lloyd Nolan delivered the eulogy on that day, January 18, 1965, on the moment of 2:00 p.m. Included was the story that Gene Raymond had never left Miss MacDonald's side during her open-heart surgery illness. On January 14, she opened her eyes for a moment, looked at her husband, and smiled wanly. "I love you," she told him. "I love you too," he replied. Then Jeanette MacDonald closed her eyes forever. Doesn't that sound like a scene from one of her movies?

One jarring note: the obliging widower, in an action meant to please his wife's loyal fans, piped her music throughout the memorial park both before and after the funeral. His selections, "Ave Maria" and "Ah, Sweet Mystery of Life" played over and over on the loudspeakers. Something went wrong with the speakers; Miss MacDonald's usual soothing soprano assaulted the mourner's ears like loud chalk scratching a blackboard.

Members of the hip hop generation and devotees of rap music surely have no acquaintance with Jeanette MacDonald who as born in Philadelphia in about 1907. (The singer zealously guarded her actual birthdate – she would never admit to being the fifty-eight years old that she actually was.)

Before sparkling operatic soprano Jeanette MacDonald first teamed with Nelson Eddy in a 1935 film musical called *Naughty Marietta*, they each were already stars. She had starred in such films as *Monte Carlo* and *One Hour With You*. He was enjoying public acclaim as a concert baritone in *Pagliacci* at the Metropolitan Opera House.

From the first duet, "Ah, Sweet Mystery of Life," on screen, the singing team was a runaway success. For eight more blockbuster films the couple serenaded American's moviegoers with thirty-six other duets. The magical twosome hit upon a hit firm formula: their faces were always meticulously made up with carefully coiffured hair. Cameras kept MacDonald and Eddy in soft focus presenting them in fuzzy but perfect screen images. The blond-haired baritone is best remembered as a Royal Canadian Mounty whereas the gussied-up soprano's rendition of "Indian Love Call" has become a staple parody of numerous female impersonators.

On March 7, 1967, two years and forty-seven days after Jeanette MacDonald's huge funeral, Nelson Eddy died. He was stricken while appearing at the Sans Souci Hotel in Hollywood, Florida. His current musical partner Gale Sherwood and his wife Ann Franklin were off stage as he suffered the stroke during a song.

When I attended the small service of Nelson Eddy, I could not help but compare it to the three-ring circus of Jeanette MacDonald. Only family, a few close friends, and several loyal fans attended the funeral at the All Saints Episcopal Church in Beverly Hills. No movie stars or celebrities were in evidence. Even fewer people attended the simple graveside burial service conducted by the Reverend J. Herbert Smith.

My Beverly Hills neighbor Eleanor Powell pointed out that the historic team of Jeanette MacDonald and Nelson Eddy was gone now, but it will never be forgotten since their music will live forever.

Eleanor Powell, the wonderful dancing star, who joined Nelson Eddy in the box office hit *Rosalie*, added, "Jeanette is now reposing at Forest Lawn (in an impressive crypt in the Hall of Freedom) and Nelson at Hollywood Memorial Cemetery (in an unimpressive grave near Rudolf Valentino's mausoleum.) Not far from Nelson is my dear mother's grave. Each week I bring roses for her, and I always place a rose at Nelson's headstone, and another for Jeanette beside his, in memory and love."

MARGARET SANDERS

She did not fear death when it came Wednesday, October 10, 2001. She had already arranged cremation for herself despite some family disapproval. At Scobee-Combs-Bowden Funeral Home in Boynton Beach, Florida, this forward-thinking woman had already planned her own memorial service. That memorial service finally took place Thursday, October 18, 2001, at 2:00 p.m. Neither she, her children, nor her grandchildren could have anticipated the overflowing crowd that came to pay their respects at the intimate family service.

Margaret Josephine Sanders, a flaming redhead, arrived March 29, 1910, squealing and kicking in Jasper, Alabama, Tallulah Bankhead's hometown. Margaret's father, Harland, was working on a railroad, on the run from Nashville to Jasper, and met her mother during an overnight stay as the train turned around in Jasper. The little girl grew up in Kentucky and Indiana while her dad went from jobs such as fireman to owner of a farm-lighting business to bankruptcy to tire salesman.

When Margaret was young, she hated her long mane of red hair. She remembers the kids shouting at her, "Redhead! Gingerhead! Five cents a cabbage head!" Now that she was a student graduating from Berea College in Kentucky, her flaming tresses often caught the attention of many young men.

Finally her father Harlan Sanders was enjoying some success running a motel/restaurant in rural Corbin, Kentucky. He worked furiously with herbs and spices to season his fried chicken.

One day in 1939 her father said, "Daughter, try this."

"I was his chief taste-tester so I swallowed the concoction," said the obedient daughter.

"You've got it!" she exclaimed.

So her father wrote the recipe for the eleven herbs and spices over the doorjam and said,

"If anything ever happens to me, that's where it is."

Thus was the beginning of the international Kentucky Fried Chicken business that reaped millions of dollars for Colonel Harland Sanders. (By the way, his Kentucky Colonel title was awarded by Governor Ruby Laffoon, a longtime fan of his delicious chicken.)

While her father's star was ascending, life for Margaret had reached rock bottom. In 1946 headstrong Margaret divorced Jimmy Adams, after fourteen years of marriage and three children. It almost became impossible for her to feed and clothe little Harland, Josephine, and Trigg. Always a seeker of truth in religion, Margaret had faith that her struggle would end – and it did.

Col. Sanders adored his eldest daughter and her three children, and was generous in sharing his newfound wealth with them. Convincing Margaret to leave her California home, he ensured her financial future by giving her the Florida franchise for Kentucky Fried Chicken as a present.

Immediately Margaret initiated carryout service in all of her KFC outlets. Soon her takeout service was copied by restaurants all over America. Next the determined daughter put a bucket on top of her outlets, plus the distinctive red and white striped awning. To be sure the Colonel was not smiling about these sweeping innovations.

Most people had a pen pal like Nancy Smith of Topeka, Kansas, or Takamitsu Masuda of Tokyo, Japan. But not Margaret Sanders – she had a running correspondence with America's greatest genius, Albert Einstein. It concerned a theory that science eventually would discover a single cosmic force behind all the different phenomena of nature. The Colonel sniffed.

Meanwhile Margaret was developing her sculpting talent underneath the Colonel's disapproving eye. Her father's comment: "Daughter, you had better leave that damn mud alone."

Margaret Sanders had a life-long interest in religion and spirituality. This search for the truth of life leads her to travel virtually all over the earth. Metaphysician-writer Joel Goldsmith appeared to be her spiritual guru. The colonel's response to all this: "Daughter, you better go to a regular church and sit in the front row."

One day Col. Harland Sanders arrived unexpectedly at his daughter's home in Florida and asked his grandchildren where their mother was. He was told that Margaret had founded the Marine Archaeological Research Society and was searching for the lost continent of Atlantis in the Bimini Islands, following the directions of psychic Edgar Cayce. This topped all of her crazy antics leading her exasperated father to shout, "Tell your mother she better get back here and attend to the business. Those people are all dead. They can't eat chicken!"

Of Margaret's sculpting talent there was never a doubt. She became internationally known as a portrait sculptor with her works both in private collections and museums. Among her commissions were sculptures of Albert Einstein, Dwight Eisenhower, Norman Rockwell and Pope Pius XII.

Even Col. Sanders reluctantly came to respect his beloved daughter as a world-class portrait sculptress. Why, he could even be found posing for her several times! One of the three bronze busts that Margaret sculpted of her father stands as his monument in a Louisville, Kentucky, cemetery. He died at age 90 in 1980.

I spoke at Magaret's 2001 memorial service. Standing next to a bronze sculpture of Col. Harland Sanders, I told the crowd about how I met the vivacious Margaret in a Los Angeles hospital back in the late 1970s. A crash through an automobile's windshield had left my entire head encased in white gauze like a mummy. Margaret walked up to me at the hospital and asked, "What is your name?"

"Buddy Galon," I responded.

"You sound Southern like me – have you ever heard of Jasper, Alabama?"

"Sure, I used to live there."

"Hush yore mouth," she squealed, "I am taking you home with me!"

After talking animatedly about life in Jasper and its native daughter Tallulah Bankhead, Margaret and I began talking about my accident.

"Where were you going when it happened?" she asked innocently.

"Well," I began, "It was Thursday evening so I was on my way to actress Beulah Bondi's house for dinner and our customary Joel Goldsmith metaphysical meeting.

"I don't believe it!" she interrupted me excitedly, "Fate, Nature, God or something brought us together. Now I <u>know</u> I am taking you home with me."

True to her word, Margaret took me home. She arranged with my doctor for me to be released for Thanksgiving; she even secured a gorgeous special duty nurse to attend to my medical needs. So on Turkey Day I actually sat down to fried chicken at Margaret's Mandeville Canyon home. At one side of me was Mrs. Clark Gable; on the other side was her young son John Clark Gable. Unexpected guests were neighbor Noah Dietrich, head of the Howard Hughes empire, and Oscar-winning actress Sissy Spacek. What a holiday to remember!

In my limited time speaking to Margaret's family and friends, I could not possibly include all the times that our lives kept touching each other. She did not know that I was the minister of the metaphysical church in Beverly Hills which she attended. We both had been associated with the Edgar Cayce Foundation of Virginia Beach, Virginia. Years later I was the minister of the metaphysical church in Palm Springs – guess who unknowingly walked in the door?

Spiritually we were totally in sync. Socially we were also two peas in a pod. While we were both living in Palm Springs, I called on Margaret to help me with fundraising for a rehabilitation facility. In a sense she assisted me in helping to found the Betty Ford Center. When we both discovered each other on the planning committee of the Bob Hope Center for Performing Arts, I promised her my solid support. After all, Margaret's handsome new husband was to design the formidable building. The colonel's daughter giggled and whispered that this was her fifth husband.

"What do you think I'm doing wrong?" she asked merrily.

I thought a minute. Then I remembered our dinner when a male hand climbed up my thigh under the table. Finally I advised, "Perhaps next time you should consider not carrying a homosexual."

To this comment, she just giggled.

In 1980 I left Palm Springs, traveled nearly three thousand miles, landing on a beautiful street called Flagler Drive in West Palm Beach, Florida. And without knowing this, who do you think also moved to this same street? Yes, Margaret lived in the clouds in the high-rise Rapallo, which looked down on my apartment.

When at last Margaret's long-awaited memoir came out, I was still making appearances with my last book BITCH. What fun we had together presenting big chunks of our rather flamboyant lives to the public! Margaret seemed tickled to shock people with stories of the Colonel's mistress in her tome, Eleven Herbs and a Spicy Daughter. Her fresh tales of the poultry prince's chicks made my book about Lady Lawford's political murder seem old hat.

No tiara, no ball gown, no endless parade of parties – this bonafide heiress to a 285 million dollar fortune left this world living life on her terms. The lady, who was the spitting image of her father, says, "We're all born with a mission. This is mine."

NICKY HILTON

"I want to marry her someday," I said to myself as the beautiful widow of Nicky Hilton walked down the aisle at his funeral. The twenty-eight-year-old brunette garbed in all black was socialite Patricia Blake McClintock. "Trish" Hilton, as she was known, had been Nicky's wife for ten years and the mother of his two sons.

When I first heard of Nicky's death, I was determined to attend the funeral. However, neighborhood gossip spread that the services would be "invitation only." Not deterred, I took down from the bookshelf The Los Angeles Blue Book, sometimes called The Social Register. It was no trouble at all to find the telephone number of Nicky's father, Conrad Hilton. Telephoning the palatial Hilton mansion, I told a servant in my best indignant aristocratic voice that my funeral invitation had obviously not been delivered. To my surprise, less than an hour after my telephone call, a staff member of the Hilton household stood at the door of my Beverly Hills home holding my funeral invitation. Leave it to me to make a silly statement: "Has Liz and Dicky arrived yet?" I suppose that I stupidly was attempting to sound as if I were on familiar terms with Elizabeth Taylor and Richard Burton.

Conrad Hilton, Nicky's father, was the source of all the money. From his buying a Texas flophouse in 1919 to eventually having the genius to establish hotel franchises abroad – Hilton was the undisputed czar of the hotel industry. However, Connie, as he was called, with all of his millions of dollars could not get accepted by old guard society. His 60-room mansion and his marriage to Hungarian actress Zsa Zsa Gabor drew attention – the wrong kind of attention. He believed purchases of the Plaza and the Waldorf-Astoria would give him prestige. Yet his crude language, constant belching, and rampant flatulence kept him from being invited to social events.

Conrad Nicholas (Nicky) Hilton, Jr., the six-foot, brown-eyed and brown-haired hotel heir, cut a wide swath in his silver and gold Mercedes-Benz convertible. Introduced by Peter Lawford at the M-G-M studio, Nicky and Elizabeth Taylor were immediately smitten with each other. Soon a storybook wedding occurred between the beautiful eighteen-year-old actress and the handsome twenty-three-year playboy.

Less than nine months after the very elaborate wedding, Elizabeth Taylor Hilton screamed "Divorce!" Insiders said the marriage failed simply because Elizabeth and Nicky were both spoiled brats. Elizabeth complained about his gambling, but admitted she liked the sex. Too, Elizabeth disliked his drinking, but admitted she liked the sex. Finally, Elizabeth abhorred his drug taking, but still admitted she liked the sex. Actress Terry Moore, who soon started dating Nicky Hilton after the breakup with Elizabeth, sang praises to Nicky's physical endowments. In her most ladylike language, Terry claimed enthusiastically, "He had absolutely the largest penis – wider than a beer can and much longer."

Nicky Hilton died of heart failure on February 5, 1969, at the age of forty-two. Conrad Hilton was a major contributor to the Church of the Good Shepherd, but tenets of Catholicism prevented his son's funeral being held there. A nearby Catholic church relaxed its strict rules allowing Nicky's funeral to be held – at a price. Poor Nicky's funeral was actually rather shabby. For sure, his casket was expensive, but it could have been better chosen. The posh flower arrangements left a lot to be desired. Was that religious elevator music being played? And where did they find that lackluster priest who conducted the service?

Perhaps the funeral was a bit on the boring side, but some of the mourners added a bit of color. Both dapper and smiling, Dean Martin and Robert Stack were consummate ushers. Conrad Hilton's girlfriend, dancer Ann Miller, was coiffed, made up, and costumed as if she were going straight from the funeral service to an M-G-M studio musical production set. I had not seen Elizabeth Taylor and Richard Burton since the premiere of their movie "The Sandpipers." She was without doubt the most beautiful woman I had ever seen, and even his pockmarked face seemed to have benefited from dermabrasion. Having arrived only a few hours earlier from their home in Gstaad, Switzerland, the Burtons attended Nicky's funeral dressed more suitable for the Snows of Kilimanjaro than the sunshine of Southern California. Oh yes, I do hope that those were sagging panty hose that Elizabeth was wearing, otherwise, she is suffering from a severe case of wrinkled legs.

At the end of the service I moved down the pew toward the church entrance. An attractive couple greeted me. I thought that I recognized her as actress Mona Freeman and her husband real estate broker Jack Ellis.

"How did you know Nicky?" Mona asked me.

"Nicky was a friend of my older brother when they were stationed together at Fort Jackson, South Carolina. With their Army buddy F. Mark Monroe IV, they used to fly in Nicky's airplane to the exclusive Palm Bay Club in Miami on weekends." I answered.

By this time Mona Freeman, her husband and I were now standing on the steps of the church when Mona asked, "You are going to the family luncheon, aren't you?" Without giving me a moment to reply, she added, "Nicky would want you there." Never one to disappoint a corpse, I agreed to go.

"Where did you park your car?" When I indicated that my yellow convertible was parked a block away, Mr. And Mrs. Ellis insisted that I join them in the waiting limousine. Only minutes later I was witness to champagne toasts to Nicky's memory. A sumptuous luncheon was served at the family-owned Beverly Hilton Hotel.

At the luncheon I spoke to pretty Trish Hilton, Nicky's widow. Who could have known her secret from the guests? Yes, she had separated from the deceased thirteen days before his death. Another secret was being hidden that day by Zsa Zsa Gabor, Nicky's stepmother. The glamorous personality confessed later, "While still married to his father, I had a love affair with Nicky. It lasted through my divorce from his father, into my marriage to actor George Sanders, and beyond Nicky's engagement to Elizabeth Taylor."

* * *

Some thirty years after Nicky Hilton's funeral, I was attending a big social event in Palm Beach. Across the room I saw a strikingly attractive brunette poured into a very fitted red fishtail gown. Her 1000-watt personality was matched by her abundant dazzling diamonds. I had once dreamed of being married to someone like her.

"Who is that gorgeous woman in red?" I asked my friend.

"That's Mrs. Horace Schmidlapp of Paris, France. Her husband was the widower of actress Carole Landis."

"Why is Mrs. Schmidlapp in Palm Beach?"

"Oh, she is visiting her daughter, Trish Hilton!"

TYRONE POWER

He was a beautiful man...Beautiful outside and
Beautiful inside. Rest well, my friend.

Cesar Romero
The Eulogy of Tyrone Power

Tyrone Edmund Power came from a family of theatrical traditions. His great-grandfather, his grandfather, and his father all were named Tyrone Power. Each was a stage actor. His mother was Shakespearean actress Patia Power who gave birth to the fourth Tyrone on May 5, 1914 in Cincinnati, Ohio.

After his early years were divided between his parents' stage and screen work in New York and Hollywood, seventeen-year-old Tyrone debuted. He was playing minor roles with a Shakespearean repertory company located in 'Chicago. His father was a senior member of the cast.

Veteran actress Katherine Cornell and her husband producer Guthrie McClintic took the young actor under their theatrical wings. After appearing with Miss Cornell on the New York stage in Romeo and Juliet and Saint Joan, Tyrone Power was signed by Twentieth-Century-Fox studio for a seven-year motion picture contract acting leading roles.

Power scored screen success in many, many films starting with Lloyds of London, and including Alexander's Ragtime Band, Rose of Washington Square, Blood and Sand revealed that Tyrone Power might be the reincarnation of Rudolf Valentino. His acting was called "perfect" by critics in the blockbuster movie The Razor's Edge. When he made Captain From Castile, Prince of Foxes, and The Black Rose, the actor bemoaned the fact that he was getting roles entirely based on the appeal of his face and physique.

In 1939 Tyrone Power married Annabelle, a lovely actress whom he met when they co-starred in the film <u>Suez</u>. That marriage was dissolved after ten years. He then wed the beautiful movie actress Linda Christian on the set of <u>Captain of Castile</u>. She was the mother of his daughters Taryn and Romina. In the last months of his life Tyrone Power married Deborah Minardos of rural Tunica, Mississippi.

After shooting a strenuous swordfight scene on the Madrid, Spain, location of his latest motion picture <u>Solomon and Sheba</u>, Tyrone Power gasped and fell unconscious. Co-star Gina Lollobrigida rushed him in her Mercedes to a clinic, but he was dead within three minutes of arrival. The date was November 15, 1958.

A memorial service was hastily arranged at the U.S. Airbase in Madrid in the presence of such fellow actors as Gina Lollobrigida, Marisa Pavan, and Jean-Pierre Aumont. George Sanders delivered an eloquent eulogy ending with "I shall always remember Tyrone Power as a man who gave more of himself than it was wise for him to give. Until in the end he gave his life." There was a military honor guard present representing the movie star's service in the armed forces. As if by magic, a special Trans World Airlines airplane whisked Tyrone Power's body back to America – compliments of his old pal, airline owner Howard Hughes.

Deborah Minardos Power, Tyrone's wife of six months, controlled firmly the Hollywood funeral. The star's two divorces prevented him from Catholic rites so the widow selected a Presbyterian Navy chaplain to conduct the service. Perhaps it was not a wise decision to insist on the small chapel at the old Hollywood Memorial Park. Henry Fonda, Yul Brynner, Gregory Peck, James Stewart, and Loretta Young were lucky enough to get seats inside the chapel. Meanwhile, scores of friends and co-workers remained outside with no seats. Then there were the hundreds of fans standing in the hot California sun.

Friends and fans grew more angry when the imperious Debbie Power refused to allow ex-wife Linda Christian and two daughters at the funeral. It is customary in Hollywood social protocol for former wives and former husbands to attend funerals discreetly. Onlookers dismissed the widow's funeral behavior as petty and ignorant. However, her negative action against Linda Christian appeared to be jealousy of a woman much more beautiful, much more talented, much more intelligent, and for being forever the mother of Tyrone Power's two daughters. By the way, a special funeral mass was held at Sacred Heart Catholic Church in Hollywood for Linda Christian and daughters Taryn and Romina. Then they flew back to their home in Paris.

In 1976 I attended the twentieth anniversary of Tyrone Power's death. Fans were milling around, visiting Rudolph Valentino and Douglas Fairbanks, Sr.'s graves. Tyrone's last wife and her entourage were huddling closely around Power's memorial bench inscribed "Good night, sweet prince" from Hamlet. Friends and fans were literally shut out.

Tyrone William Power IV, the son that the movie star did not live to see, apparently did not attend his father's anniversary. As handsome as his dad, young Ty had been appearing in a college production of Macbeth, thus beginning a new chapter in the 150-year career that the First Tyrone Power had begun.

Rumors abound that Deborah Menardos Power and her young son have feuded and are not speaking. Incidentally, since Tyrone Power's death his widow has married movie mogul Arthur Loew, Jr. She divorced him and wed his cousin, David Lawrence. They now live in Mexico.

COUNTESS MONIQUE
DU BOISROUVRAY

Nearly fifty of us sat in a collection of 300 species of rare palms. Eight monumental brick sculptures stood to the left and to the right more than 100 works of art were displayed. This dramatic dense foliage reminiscent of ancient jungle civilizations was the unique setting for the unique memorial service for the unique Countess Monique du Boisrouvray.

I first met Countess Monique several years ago when our mutual friend, His Serene Highness Prince Franz Josef Antony zu Hohenlohe Waldenburg-Schillingfurst of Vienna, Austria, introduced us outside her living place in West Palm Beach, Florida. "Franzi," as we called the prince, continued to be the touchstone of our acquaintanceship.

Born in 1920 in France, Madame du Boisrouvray's earlier life revolved around the art world and European society. After her marriage to accomplished musician count Henri du Boisrouvray, the couple founded a highly successful music festival in Spain.

While visiting friends in Palm Beach, Madame du Boisrouvray met and subsequently became the close friend of the prominent artist-sculptor Ann Norton. Mrs. Norton's artistic vision soon became Countess Monique's artistic vision.

When Robert Hubbard Norton, the founder of the widely-acclaimed Norton Museum of Art, died, the French noblewoman then became the devoted companion of his widow. Nepal and India was home-away-from-home for the two women. Extensive stays in both countries led to Countess du Boisrouvray's long friendship with the famed spiritual leader, the Dalai Lama. (Never mind her devout Catholicism!)

Ann Weaver Norton died in 1982. It was her specific request that her staunchest supporter Madame du Boisrouvray was to continue living in the Norton home at 253 Barcelona Road. Mrs. Norton knew that her friend would be the most ardent leader in support of the newly-established public foundation, the Ann Norton Sculpture Gardens. However, the deceased artist-sculptor probably could not have imagined that trustees of the sculpture gardens and other members of the local art community would attempt to toss Madame du Boisrouvray into the street. Not only that, but they also tried to sever the countess' leadership role in the public foundation. Never try to dismiss a redhead! The fiery flame-haired noblewoman not only bested her adversaries in a well-publicized battle but also, for the rest of her life, she was fiercely devoted to the cause of the Ann Norton Sculpture Gardens. Her passionate support remained absolutely undiminished to her very end.

Countess Monique du Boisrouvray opened her door with loving kindness and warm hospitality to all – whether it be a local student interested in botany or directors from the Metropolitan Museum of Art or a curious neighborhood housewife or officers from the Guggenheim Museum.

Anne, the Marquise de Rochambeau of Paris, survived her sister. Countess Albina du Boisrouvray, the noted Parisian philanthropist, survived her aunt. Prince Rainier of Monaco also was a survivor of his first cousin.

So as we sat in front of that huge brick sculpture with its six sprays of flowers and two colored photographs, we lowered our heads in prayer. A cherub-faced young priest, garbed in all white, led the upbeat memorial service. Missing were the deceased's great friends, the Tibetan monks. One by one, seven of the countess' good friends stood before the motley group each endeavoring to recount special remembrances.

A glass of French champagne ended our formal goodbye at the intimate memorial of Countess Monique du Boisrouvray held in the Ann Norton Sculpture Gardens. By the way, the date is February 10, 2001 – Madame du Boisrouvray's birthday.

PERRY COMO

In Memory of
PERRY COMO
Born
May 18, 1912
Died
May 12, 2001

Perry left Jupiter, Florida and his many fans on May 12, to join his beloved wife, Roselle, for Mother's Day and together they are celebrating his birthday.

The above words were printed on a card bearing an autographed picture of Perry Como. At both the memorial wake and the funeral these cards were presented to the mourners.

Quiet, cool, soft-spoken, laid-back entertainer Perry Como would possibly have turned over in his grave if he had known that his estate would cause a controversial public dispute of his family.

First, within months of his death after a long struggle with Alzheimer's disease, Perry Como's sacred living place was opened to the public. "It was a home built in 1957 at the Jupiter Inlet Colony of which the cardigan-clad singer had once said, "The world that fussed over Perry Como never made it through the front door."

It is somewhat sad to note that the world can now get through that door – Perry Como's privacy is a thing of the past. For about four million dollars Waterfront Properties offered to see the 5,755-square-foot home situated on Florida's Intracoastal Waterway.

Going once; going twice; sold to the bidder in the green baseball cap. A box of old boots sold for $3,500. One of Como's sweaters brought $1,600. A 1999 Cadillac went for $18,000. Why, Dawson's Auctioneers and Appraisers could even provide any die-hard Perry Como fan with an eggbeater or a toothbrush!

Como had directed that his three children and their families receive the most important items in his house. All other belongings were to be sold at auction. However, did he mean for his most private and personal things to become objects of public consumption? And what about the proposed Perry Como Museum? The auctioning of more than 1500 items to the public greatly limited the future museum's memorabilia collection.

The three children – Ronald Como of Granger, Indiana; David Como of San Francisco, California, and Therese Thibadeau of Jupiter, Florida – feuded over their father's estate. Before they finally reached agreement, they were literally fighting over 200 pieces of the entertainer's memorabilia, including his gifts from Pope XII. A battle over Perry Como's health care and living will erupted. The daughter also tried to get her brother Ronald removed as the estate's executor by reason of mental stability.

Born Pierino Roland Como on May 18, 1912, in Canonsburg, Pennsylvania, Perry Como was the seventh son of a seventh son. By the time he was twelve years of age he was apprenticed as a barber in the small mining town. Then Como, age 14, took over an established barbering business.

1933 was an important year in Perry Como's life. He sold his haircutting business to become a singer with the Freddy Carlone band in Cleveland. It was this same year that he married his high school sweetheart Roselle Beline. The marriage lasted sixty-five years, until her death in 1998 at age 84.

After a stint with Ted Weems' Orchestra, Como landed his own radio show on CBS in 1943. A recording contract with RCA followed and before long the singer had his first number one hit, "Till The End of Time."

Starting with the mid-1950s, Perry Como began thirty years of television that made him virtually an American household entertainment staple. Famous for his cardigan sweaters and his smooth melodic singing style, Como through the years recorded such hits as "And I Love You So," "Hot Diggity," "Catch a Falling Star," "Papa Loves Mambo," and "It's Impossible."

About 750 people attended the funeral mass at 10:30 a.m. May 19, 2001 at Saint Edward's Catholic Church, Palm Beach, Florida. The service was a celebration of the life of Perry Como, his faith and family.

Eleven priests were banked at the altar by cream-colored flowers. Cantor Marilyn Coscia made the rafters ring with her stirring rendition of "Ave Maria." A message was read from Bishop Anthony J. O'Connell calling Como "one of God's greatest gift."

As I sat on the left side of the church near the back, I suddenly realized that I was sitting in the exact same seat that I had sat in at Rose Kennedy's funeral.

Entertainer Perry Como left this world at Friday's service with both beautiful music and his usual standing-room-only crowd.

ROD LaROCQUE

On so many occasions Beulah Bondi, often called America's premier character actress, asked me to escort her to various events. After all, we were neighbors and good friends despite our age difference.

One such special event to which I escorted Beulah was a private preview of the Los Angeles Art Association's current exhibit. By the way, the ultra-dignified Miss Bondi was a member of the prestigious board of directors.

The host-actor-art connoisseur Edward G. Robinson greeted us at the locked door with champagne. Beulah's ice-blue brocade suit designed by Irene Sharif and her rare Baroque pearls were greatly admired, but nobody seemed to be taken with my simple black tuxedo.

Anyway, the exhibit was composed of modern art, and I grew bored very quickly. It appeared to me that eyes were painted where the stomach should be, and the most praised artwork seemed to be cucumbers kneeling in prayer. Looking around the museum and estimating the average age of the art patrons to be eighty, I said wearily to Beulah:

"Every one from the old days of Hollywood is here except Rod LaRocque and Vilma Banky."

"Excuse me, young man," the distinguished man corrected me, "My name is pronounced LaRocque, like a rock...Hello Beulah dear, how are you?...By the way, young man, it was kind of you to mention my wife Vilma...she is at home not feeling too well."

I stood there stunned. I was bored with the art exhibit and casually uttered to Beulah two names that I had memorized as I strolled down the Walk of Fame on Hollywood Boulevard, and accidentally the man I offhandedly mentioned was standing at my elbow. That is strange!

Of course, Beulah properly introduced me to Rod LaRocque, and the rest of the evening Rod entertained me greatly. Still under the impression that I knew who he was, Rod enthralled me with colorful tales of his and Vilma's reign during silent pictures. What a wonderful story he told me about his and beautiful Vilma's big Hollywood wedding! By the end of the evening Rod and I were on the way to becoming fast friends.

Sometime later Beulah Bondi called me, "Did you read about Rod LaRocque's death in the morning newspaper? Would you be so kind as to escort me to the funeral?"

"But I can't go – it's a private funeral for invited guests only," I protested.

"Buddy dear," Beulah sweetly responded, "Rod placed your name on his funeral guest list before he died."

Pierce Brothers Mortuary arranged the private service in Beverly Hills for actor Rod LaRocque. He was age 70 when he died of a brief illness at his home.

LaRocque, the handsome hero star of the silent film extravaganza "The Ten Commandments" and the sound picture blockbuster "The Hunchback of Notre Dame," had a career that literally spanned motion picture history.

Perhaps the biggest wedding ever in Hollywood was the union of matinee idol Rod LaRocque and Hungarian actress Vilky Banky. Studio boss Louis B. Mayer financed it; director Cecil B. DeMille served as the best man; film studio head Samuel Goldwyn gave the bride away. Who can ever forget the arrival at Rod and Vilma's wedding of western star Tom Mix? He was in a coach pulled by four white horses with a cloud of trailing white ostrich feathers. Thousands of fans applauded.

Rod LaRocque's funeral was a truly dignified funeral for a truly dignified man. However, I don't feel the dignified Beulah Bondi forgave me for driving her to the service that day in my very undignified red convertible sports car with the top down.

GEORGE REEVES

I never believed much in levitation. The illusion of raising and keeping a body or object in the air with little or no physical contact did not particularly interest me. After all, was it a part of mysticism or the laws of gravity? Magic or plain old hocus-pocus?

It was in the late 1960s that I was a guest in a Spanish-style stucco Beverly Hills, California, tract house that would probably sell for over a million dollars. Neighbors claimed that M-G-M songstress Deanna Durbin had once lived there.

Entering the living room after spending the evening enjoying the nightclub act of mentalist Criswell, the group dispersed to various parts of the large room. Two blonde-haired, stylishly-dressed ladies plopped down on the carpeted floor with their legs extended carefully under a large glass-topped table. If one looked more closely, one might decide the ladies were twins, and close to eighty years old, although they appeared at least twenty years younger.

Behind one of the ladies sat a bald-headed man who was holding her small poodle. He was what was considered a "Beverly Hills walker." In those days I was unaware of the meaning of the term "walker." Now I think of a walker as a younger man who usually escorts older women in a non-intimate relationship based mostly on her money. He may be educated, well-dressed, a good dancer, and is often a homosexual. Imagine my surprise later when I was at a party honoring the First Lady Nancy Reagan and she was escorted by her "walker," Jerome Zipkin!

"Oh, let's contact George Reeves!" shouted one of the twins with glee.

"Yes, let's bring George back. That will be such fun," chimed in the other twin.

Before I had a chance to protest, I found myself sitting on the floor, legs sprawled under the huge wrought iron coffee table, sandwiched between the animated twins.

"George Reeves. Who the heck was this George Reeves that the ladies were talking about?" I muttered to myself. Then all of a sudden I remembered my friends Peter Dane and Robert Osborne talking about an actor named George Reeves. The two film buffs mentioned that he was one of the red-haired Tarleton brothers who wooed Scarlett O'Hara in "Gone With The Wind." They also pointed out that Reeves starred in the motion picture "So Proudly We Hail" opposite Claudette Colbert.

Bingo! It came to me – I know who George Reeves is. He was that guy who played Superman and died a bizarre death.

Sitting at the other end of the long glass coffee table, facing me was a stunning woman with a flaming crown of red hair. Her classic turquoise dress was adorned with a very large diamond pin. The woman was the daughter of one of the energetic twin ladies. Oh, and I also found out that the striking redhead was the former Mrs. George Reeves!

While we were waiting to begin the levitation session, the bright, witty twins, who were forever blondes, chatted idly away. I overheard them talking about whether or not Toni Mannix, the rich "broad" who "kept" George Reeves, had him murdered. The other twin disagreed: "No, I think that it was that bad-tempered party girl Lenore Lemon, who was engaged to him, that killed him. After all, she was in his house when he died."

The ex-Mrs. George Reeves, who had divorced the actor in 1949 after ten years of marriage, did not seem to be sharing her mother and aunt's glee in discussing her former husband's untimely demise. In fact, she remained serious, saying only that George was a weak man.

Meanwhile, the twins were exuberant at the possibility of communicating with the dead, especially someone that had actually been a relative. During the entire ten-minute levitation process, I did not ask a single question of George Reeves. Opposite me, the very solemn ex-wife only asked one question: "George, are you happier where you are today?" All of the rest of the questions for the deceased actor came from the joyful twins. Their questions were like the following:

(1) Did you like wearing tights with your Superman costume? Were those rubber muscles you wore hot?
(2) Are you gay? Your intimate association with rampant homosexual Gilmore Brown, Pasadena Playhouse director, implicated this.

(3) George, you didn't really go up to your bedroom, rip off all of your clothes, and jump from your second floor window in a Superman suicide attempt, did you?

(4) Get real. I know that you had a .38 caliber bullet in your head, but how did those two extra bullets get in the wall?

(5) What roles did Toni Mannix and Lenore Lemon have in your death on June 16, 1959?

(6) Is it true that your body was not buried but rather kept in refrigeration for several years while three different women were in the legal courts claiming your body?

(7) Actress Susan Strasberg moved into your Benedict Canyon home in Los Angeles. Is it true – as she says – that you return to that house often?

Numbly I said my pleasantries to my host and hostess as I stumbled into the pleasant night air. I sat in my convertible without switching the ignition on still in a cloud from the evening's activities. Did I see the heavy glass table levitate through the air? Yes, I thought so. Did I hear strange noises and voices coming from nowhere? Again I thought so. As I drove off into the glistening stars of a Hollywood sky, I accepted the fact that there were just some things that I would never understand.

THE DEATHLY DUO

"Hello, this is Jim calling from Palm Springs. Are you still driving in from Santa Barbara to meet Michaelanne and me early this evening?"

"Yeah, sure. I've completed the lyrics on the first ballad, and I've composed some dynamite music for the overture." I said enthusiastically.

"Whoa, whoa!" Jim cut me off. "No work tonight." Michaelanne and I are hosting a black-tie formal sit-down dinner for our closest friends. Hurry on down."

"Will you make my favorite hors'deuves, Jim?"

"What one is that?"

"The one Beulah Bondi taught you – raw button mushrooms stuffed with Beluga caviar. Okay?"

"Oh, okay. See you tonight. Bye."

"See ya, bye" I ended the telephone conversation.

Jim and I had been boyhood chums, both of us living near Panama City, Florida, where each of our fathers was a Southern Baptist minister. Our college years and early careers led us down separate paths, but we were unexpectedly reunited years later nearly three thousand miles away in Palm Springs, California. There I walked into his office where he was director of the regional theatre. Immediately picking up our friendship from the past, we soon were working together on projects of mutual interest. Together Jim and I collaborated on theatrical productions and film festivals along with serving on the planning committees of the Betty Ford Center and the Bob Hope Center for Performing Arts. Of the many things that Jim accomplished, I was most impressed with his nomination for the Pulitzer Prize in literature.

Michaelanne was a relatively new friend to me. First I knew her to be Jim's intimate companion. Next I knew her to be a talented actress who was divorced from an unsuccessful actor with whom she had a teenaged son. Finally I knew her to be secretly depressed and on medication although outwardly she appeared vivacious and full of ambition.

Genius, a rollicking comedy, was what brought Jim, Michaelanne, and me together anew. The three of us received permission from Patrick Dennis (author of Auntie Mame) to transform his Genius from a book to a musical comedy play. Thus, every weekend I would come in from my new place in Santa Barbara and Jim would drive in from Palm Springs; we would converge upon Michaelanne's Hollywood home to collaborate on our collaborative effort.

On the afternoon of Jim and Michaelanne's dinner party, I luckily sped through Los Angeles' Friday afternoon heavy traffic. At exactly 5:45 p.m. I called Michaelanne's home to offer to pick up anything for the dinner when I came over.

"Hello," I said when the receiver was lifted.

Silence.

"May I speak to Jim?"

Again silence – then an abrupt "no."

Jokingly I said, "Oh, Jim will do anything to keep from making my favorite hors 'deuves!"

"Jim is dead and mama is too," blurted out Michaelanne's young son.

The next voice I heard was a L.A. police officer saying "no information" before hanging up the telephone.

I rushed to Michaelanne's home in time to see several police officers, the medical examiner, and two covered bodies all leaving the premises. The totally distraught son of Michaelanne, who had discovered the bodies of Jim and his mother on the bathroom floor, was taken to the home of a relative.

Inside the house I was completely alone. I began searching for a guest list for the formal dinner party that was scheduled to begin in only one hour. It was nowhere to be found. Since I couldn't find a list, I couldn't notify the invited guests.

Instead, I placed Jim's favorite armchair at an angle in front of the fireplace. Bringing in the old battered Royal typewriter that he wrote his Pulitzer Prize material on, I placed it in the seat of the chair. Then I arranged Michaelanne's favorite armchair opposite Jim's. In her chair I placed the red feather boa that she had worn in her favorite stage role, Auntie Mame.

Dressed in my tuxedo, I greeted each guest as they arrived. Serving them flutes of Dom Perignon champagne, I chatted lightheartedly without giving any explanation of the host and hostess' absences. However, I almost lost my composure when I saw the raw button mushrooms stuffed with Beluga caviar that Jim must have prepared just for me before the double suicide.

After the most delicious meal, I assembled the guests in the beautifully decorated living room. I addressed the group: "Michaelanne and Jim, who are our dear friends, could not be with us tonight in person. However, the typewriter and red boa symbolizes their presence. Please try to understand that earlier this afternoon they chose to begin another part of their lives. They would want you to support their decisions and wish them well."

For nearly two hours the invited guests laughed and cried as stories of the absent couple were told, making it a truly unusual event.

DR. HUBERT EATON

"THE GREATEST FUNERAL OF ALL TIME!" was the united opinion of the 1000 invited guests at the September 26, 1966, memorial service of Dr. Hubert Eaton, the founder of Forest Lawn.

Born in 1881 in rural Missouri, Hubert Lewright Eaton was a neighborhood schoolmate of Harry S. Truman, future president of the United States. Eaton Later majored in science at William Jewell College in Liberty, Missouri.

Subsequently Eaton as a young man became a cow puncher. He even served his country in the military, quelling riots in Mexico. When Eaton mined silver in the Nevada silver field, he suddenly stuck it rich.

What goes up must come down, so when the silver streak dried up, Eaton found himself not only broke but also deeply in debt.

Busted and down on his luck, Hubert Eaton in 1912 finally found a job in Tropico, California, a dusty suburb of Los Angeles. Incidentally, the little town of Tropico later changed its name to Glendale. Eaton's new job was selling burial plots in a dreary twelve-acre cemetery called Forest Lawn.

Eaton had found his challenge. In his first year he introduced his "pre-need" plan to California newcomers. This concept increased sales by 250% saving the business from possible bankruptcy. Soon he bought an interest in the cemetery.

By New Year's Day of 1917, Eaton's dream was on its way to fruition. Just like in a Frank Capra motion picture, the thirty-six-year-old cemetery plot salesman was standing on a hilltop overlooking Forest Lawn when a vision came to him. First, he would expand the cemetery to fifty-five acres. He envisioned narrow, winding roads meandering through lush green grass and magnificent trees. He wanted to offer birth-to-death services including baptisms, weddings, and funerals. Oh yes, he also desired a respected Board of Regents.

At that time Hubert Eaton said, "The cemeteries of today are wrong, because they depict an end, not a beginning."

By New Year's Day, 1934, nearly two decades after Eaton's vision, he was able to see his dream coming rue. He had transformed the tiny graveyard into a beautiful 300-acre memorial park for the living. For aesthetic purposes, he had standing tombstones converted to ground-level bronze plaques. Finally, Forest Lawn now offered everything in one place – mortuary, cemetery, church, and flower shop.

I was appearing as an entertainer at a popular Beverly Hills bistro called Frascati's Gourmet back in the late 1960s. Dr. Hubert Eaton, recently retired to 837 Greenway Drive, Beverly Hills, and would often be in my audience. I especially remember one Sunday evening when Dr. Eaton came up to request "Born Free" while I was doing a hectic balancing act between my front room show dueting with Debbie Reynolds on "Abba Dabba Honeymoon" and my back room music, "Arriverderci Roma," for Hedy LaMarr's divorce party from oilman Howard Lee.

By the time of Eaton's death in 1966, one and a half million visitors a day were enjoying Forest Lawn's spiritual haven for the living, with the re-creation of famous churches and fine art reproductions. Potential customers, of course, were introduced to one-stop funeral service: mortuary, cemetery, church and flower shop.

Because of Hubert Eaton's revolutionizing of the funeral industry, thousands of people took advantage of his "buy now, pay later" concept. Many people were taken with the celebrity angle. After all, nearby Hollywood was providing Forest Lawn with some glittering permanent residents. The idea that an ordinary person could spend the Great Hereafter with their favorite movie star had great appeal for some customers.

The Wee Kirk o' the Heather, another of Eaton's dreams, is a reproduction of the small 14th century Scottish church where Annie Laurie, the sweetheart of poet Robert Burns, worshipped. Ronald Reagon and Jane Wyman were married in the quaint chapel and both humorist Will Rogers and platinum blonde actress Jean Harlow had funeral services there. Do you remember when English author Evelyn Waugh poked fun at Forest Lawn in the book that became the motion picture "The Loved One"?

Hubert Lewright Eaton took his last breath at about 5 o'clock in the evening September 20, 1966. When I went to the visitation a few nights later, I was not disappointed by the grandeur of it all. Following Dr. Eaton's pre-need instructions, the expensive bronze casket seemed to be floating on one Greek marble column. Behind the casket was the impressively huge Leonardo da Vinci's "The Last Supper," re-created in stained glass. Soft pink lighting bathed the entire funeral scene while symphonic music emanated from a hidden sound system.

Red velvet ropes prevented mourners from too close a peek at the reposing Eaton. Writer Jessica Mitford would probably say the 85-year-old corpse had been "sprayed, sliced, pierced, pickled, trussed, trimmed, creamed, waxed, painted, rouged, and finally dressed" transforming him into the perfect picture of a baby's bottom. The last time I saw a face as tight and as unlined – it was on actress Loretta Young!

As I drove my yellow convertible through the winding roads of Forest Lawn Memorial Park of Glendale on September 26, 1966, I marveled at the beauty. On the right was the 25-foot reproduction statue of Michelangelo's "David;" other marble sculptures as well as large mosaics were on my left.

I stopped in front of the massive Hall of the Crucifixion and Resurrection located on the memorial park's highest hill. Hundreds of expensive floral arrangements blocked the entrance and all of the walkways. One enormous church created of thousands of flowers was more suitable for a Rose Parade float. A well-dressed woman near me said to her husband upon viewing the outrageous flower-bedecked church, "We've lived in smaller apartments than that!"

The funeral of Hubert Eaton was attended by 1000 invitation-only business and cultural leaders. As I surveyed the crowd, I saw such luminaries as actress Greer Garson, Comedian Joe E. Brown, publisher George Randolph Hearst, Herbert Hoover, Jr. and Walt Disney. Even President Richard Nixon, unable to attend, sent a message of condolence.

The hundreds of Forest Lawn employees formed an honor guard. As the ceremony began, they lined the corridors and the walls while majestic pipe organ music rattled the windows. In paraded eighteen regents to the front of the hall dressed in flowing red robes and what looked like red sailor caps.

After a stirring rendition of "Ah, Sweet Mystery of Life" by a local Irish tenor, the governor of California Goodwin Knight delivered the eulogy. However, it was the simple but eloquent words of future president Ronald Reagan that truly brought tears to the eyes of the mourners.

The end of the funeral service featured two famous choirs performing Handel's stirring "Hallelujah Chorus" in union. As the singing became higher pitched, suddenly the curtain unfurled on the world's largest religious painting. Then, as the music began to reach its bombastic climax, a hydraulic lift seemed to raise Hubert Eaton's casket upward while, from the heavens above, rose petals floated down to kiss the founder of Forest Lawn.

Eaton was interred in the Great Mausoleum, under the Last Supper Window, the prime spot that he picked for himself.

Before joining his customers in eternity, Hubert Eaton laid out plans of his last vision. Today there are five Forest Lawn memorial parks – Glendale, Hollywood Hills, Cypress, Covina Hills, and Long Beach. They are unrivaled in celebrity clientele and second only to the Arlington National Cemetery as a tourist attraction.

P.S. AS we drove home from the extravaganza, I asked my friend, actor Richard Brian, what his thoughts were on the unusual funeral. In his deep baritone voice, he spurted out, "Aw shit, Bud, I didn't know whether to shed tears for the dead guy or give a standing ovation for his Hollywood production!"

ABOUT THE AUTHOR

The author divides his life between residences in Beverly Hills and Palm Springs, California, and Palm Beach, Florida. While a graduate student at UCLA, Buddy Galon became known as a top society entertainer and a Hollywood gossip columnist for newspapers. Later he distinguished himself as a director for children on stage, television, and in motion pictures.